P9-CCW-893

Islamophobia

Islamophobia

Making Muslims the Enemy

Peter Gottschalk and
Gabriel Greenberg

ROWMAN & LITTLEFIELD PUBLISHERS, INC.
Lanham • Boulder • New York • Toronto • Plymouth, UK

ROWMAN & LITTLEFIELD PUBLISHERS, INC.

Published in the United States of America
by Rowman & Littlefield Publishers, Inc.
A wholly owned subsidiary of The Rowman & Littlefield Publishing Group, Inc.
4501 Forbes Boulevard, Suite 200, Lanham, Maryland 20706
www.rowmanlittlefield.com

Estover Road
Plymouth PL6 7PY
United Kingdom

British Library Cataloguing in Publication Information Available

Library of Congress Cataloging-in-Publication Data:

Gottschalk, Peter, 1963-
Islamophobia : making Muslims the enemy / Peter Gottshalk and Gabriel
Greenberg.
p. cm.
Includes bibliographical references and index.
ISBN-13: 978–0-7425–5286–9 (cloth : alk. paper)
ISBN-10: 0–7425–5286–1 (cloth : alk. paper)
1. Muslims—United States—Caricatures and cartoons. 2. Stereotypes (Social
psychology)—United States—Caricatures and cartoons. 3. United States—Ethnic
relations—Caricatures and cartoons. 4. Muslims in popular culture—United States.
5. Muslims—United States—Public opinion. 6. Islam—United States—Public
opinion. 7. Public opinion—United States. 8. Stereotypes (Social psychology)—
United States. 9. United States—Ethnic relations. 10. American wit and humor,
Pictorial. I. Greenberg, Gabriel, 1981- II. Title.
E184.M88G68 2008
305.6'970973—dc22

2007004887

Printed in the United States of America

©™ The paper used in this publication meets the minimum requirements of
American National Standard for Information Sciences—Permanence of Paper
for Printed Library Materials, ANSI/NISO Z39.48-1992.

Gabriel Greenberg dedicates this book
to all of my teachers.

Peter Gottschalk dedicates this book
to Ari, my daughter and inspiration.

Contents

Acknowledgments

$\mathscr{T}$he seed for this book was sown in a slide lecture by Professor John Woods at the University of Chicago. Inspired by Sam Keen's *Faces of the Enemy*, this lecture discussed the portrayal of Muslims and Islam in American political cartoons. Peter, in the audience as a graduate student, left motivated to include political cartoons in his own classes once he began to teach. When he did, it helped inform the interest of Gabriel, who investigated the topic in his senior honors thesis. For both, Keen's book provided useful insights and illustrative examples for their own research.

Both authors are indebted to Wesleyan University, which provided funds to defray the copyright costs of publishing the cartoons included in the volume. Special thanks go to Dean Don Moon for his unwavering support. We also acknowledge the important insights contributed by members of the Wesleyan University community to this project during its formative stages, especially Bruce Masters. Both of us are under a great debt of obligation to Rhonda Kissinger and, especially, Millie Hunter, who worked so hard tracking down and obtaining the permissions necessary for the volume, and Allyn Wilkinson and Kendall Hobbs for their help with the cartoons. Beyond Wesleyan, we appreciate Carl Ernst for his comments, Bruce Lawrence for his insights, and John Esposito for his support.

Gabriel would personally like to offer thanks to his family and his professors at Wesleyan, especially Vijay Pinch, who prodded me toward a love of history and knowing; Vera Schwarcz for her compassionate approach to understanding; and Peter Gottschalk, who inspired this work through his commitment to revealing to us what it is we think. Peter has much to teach about tolerance and coexistence, and I am a proud (yet work-in-progress) product of that education.

Peter would like to acknowledge his father, Rudolf Gottschalk, and his friend Phil Hopkins for their invaluable and insightful editorial comments and suggestions. Shannon Winnubst deserves particular thanks for her encouragement to pursue this project. I also appreciate the insights offered by faculty and students at Wesleyan University and Southwestern University with whom I have had the privilege of sharing my thoughts on these matters and who prove the adage that we are all teachers of one another. Of course, Gabe Greenberg deserves my deepest appreciation for working with me. This book results directly from his interest, which nurtured the nascent project; his research, which established its historical roots; and his outstanding writing and editing, which brought it to fruition. Finally, and always first, I acknowledge the inestimable support of my mother and the rest of my family during the difficult days of this work's composition, and the exuberant presence of my daughter, Ari, in my life and work: Writing remains lifeless without love.

Introduction

$\mathcal{T}$he controversy regarding the Danish publication of editorial cartoons negatively depicting the Prophet Muhammad rages outside our walls even as we prepare this book for publication. Not only does the unfortunately fatal conflict demonstrate the dynamics we identify as Islamophobia, it also demonstrates the seriousness with which political cartoons can be taken.

The issue originated with twelve depictions of the Prophet Muhammad commissioned by the culture editor of the Danish newspaper *Jyllands-Posten*. He had noticed a hesitancy among Europeans in their portrayals of Islam.[1] A Dutch Muslim, offended by the images published in September 2005, sought redress from the newspaper and the government but found none. At his prompting, eleven ambassadors of Muslim-majority nations asked for a meeting with the government, which turned down their request. He then turned to the scholars of al-Azhar University in Cairo and the secretary general of the Arab League in Lebanon, who condemned the images.[2] Finally, awareness of the cartoons became widespread after they made the rounds at an Islamic conference in Mecca.[3] A global protest soon grew, typified by peaceful gatherings of thousands of protestors in many places but overshadowed by violence in Damascus, Beirut, Tehran, Kabul, Lahore, and Benghazi.

Once more the familiar pattern had unfolded, as some Muslims reacted violently to an apparently insignificant event that seemed the latest battlefront in the West's holding action to preserve inalienable rights against ever-threatening Islamic intolerance. Although the Muslims involved never represented more than a fraction of a fraction of the world's more than one billion Muslims, their vociferous fury only confirmed a

1

Western image of Muslim intolerance and Islamic otherness. The media's consistent disinterest in nonviolent Muslim perspectives hardened this view. The perception of this conclusion, already familiar to many Muslims in the West and elsewhere, alienates ever more Muslims. Where the spiral ends, no one knows—but it doesn't appear promising.

This particular controversy perfectly illuminates the multiple aspects of these larger issues. The widespread puzzlement among non-Muslim Americans about the sharp responses reflects how little they understand Muslims. The breadth of Muslim response demonstrates both a heightened sensitivity to Western denigration of Islam and an increasing sense that the West seeks a war against Muslims through either constant deprecation, as in the cartoon controversy, or outright conquest, as in Afghanistan and Iraq. All of this turns wildly on the fulcrum of asymmetrical power. Muslims in the West and elsewhere know that now, as has been the case since the era when European imperialists ruled over most Muslims, what they think about Christians has far fewer consequences than what Westerners think about Muslims. With each passing skirmish, Muslims characterize these Western thoughts as Islamophobia. Simultaneously, the predominantly Christian and/or secular populations of the West do not appreciate that their attitudes toward Islam both presume the norms of Christianity and secularism and negatively reflect centuries of religious and political conflict around the world.

Ultimately, very few on either side wish to pick a fight. Yet the distance between the various perspectives involved allows some to opportunistically manipulate Islamophobia for their own advancement. The Danish editor, disagreeing with the hesitancy of some Europeans to offend, deliberately defied Muslim sensitivities. The Syrian government doubtlessly allowed, and in fact may have promoted, the burning of the Danish and Norwegian embassies to serve its own political ends. Sadly, dozens of people have died because of the agitations, while political fissures and social stereotypes have deepened.

Despite the rhetoric, no essential difference underlies imagined Western and Islamic civilizations. In fact, three years before the current controversy the same editor for *Jyllands-Posten* turned down cartoons satirizing the resurrection of Jesus because it would "provoke an outcry" among Christians. In his own defense, he argued that that case differed because he had not commissioned the images.[4] This demonstrates exactly how some Westerners perceive a radical difference between themselves and Muslims when, with regard to this issue, none exists. The editor obviously recognized that members of both Muslim and Christian Danish communities might object to negative caricatures of their most important figures. However, whereas he voluntarily censored himself in deference to Christians, he deliberately provoked the outrage of Muslims in order to protest the self-censorship of those deferring to this group. Clearly, in his view, Muslims represented a threat in the same scenario in which Christians did not. Islamophobia—enacted by Westerners and perceived by Muslims—plays a critically central role in convincing many that a civilizational clash will be inevitable and all-consuming by establishing the "fact" of an essential and irreconcilable difference between "them" and "us."

If you are skeptical about the notion of "Islamophobia," get a piece of paper and brainstorm. Write down, with as little thought and as much honesty as possible, all the words that come to mind when you think of the words "Islam" or "Muslim." What names, places, events, ideas, practices, and objects do you associate with these terms?[5]

Most Americans who we have asked to do this exercise have given an almost routine set of answers. The names and events they think of tend to be associated with violence (e.g., Osama bin Laden, the 9/11 tragedies, Palestinian suicide bombers), the ideas and practices associated with oppression (e.g., jihad, veiling, Islamic law), and the places limited to the Middle East (e.g., Saudi Arabia, Iraq, Iran). To be sure, some answers escape this pattern (e.g., boxer Muhammad Ali, pilgrimage to Mecca, the Quran), but these are relatively few. When asked about their answers, many Americans respond that, unfortunate as such associations may be, Muslims and Islam feature prominently in many of the world's conflicts and injustices. And this, they often conclude, reflects something inherent about the religion and its associated cultures. Judging from portrayals of Islam and Muslims in the American media, it's hard to argue with them.

However, these answers seem less certain in the face of certain facts. For instance, more Muslims live east of Afghanistan than west of it, rendering the Middle East a demographically minor place in "the Muslim world" relative to South and Southeast Asia. The nations with the most Muslims are, in order, Indonesia, Pakistan, India, and Bangladesh. Although the numbers can only be estimated, at least 1.2 billion people identify themselves as Muslim globally—that is, one in five people. The majority of these Muslims do not participate in political violence, and few aspire to establish an Islamic state in their own country, let alone force one upon others. Almost all of these Muslims live under civil laws fashioned after Western models and relatively few seek to replace these with sharia (Islamic law). If the case were otherwise, the world would be incalculably more convulsed than it is.

The question, then, is how, in the minds of so many Americans, has Islam become synonymous with the Middle East, Muslim men with violence, and Muslim women with oppression? The answer points to a history—as old as Islam itself—of confrontation between an overwhelmingly Christian Europe and predominantly Muslim Middle East over economic resources, political power, and religious sites. Or so it would be portrayed; in fact, the antagonists never represented a united Europe or Middle East and often battled among their coreligionists as much as against their supposed enemies. As this competition unfolded (often enough, until the last two centuries, unfavorably for Europeans), Europeans came to negatively portray Muslims so effectively and so universally that the terms "Islam" and "Muslim" have come to inherently evoke suspicion and fear on the part of many.

These are the roots of Islamophobia.

One measure of the significance of this phenomenon is the tenacity of its stereotypes. Despite more than a half century of both economic dependence on Middle Eastern oil and political involvement in Middle Eastern affairs, American images and understandings of Middle Eastern cultures remain largely unchanged. From the package for Camel cigarettes to the decor of the Trump Taj Mahal Casino in Atlantic City, pyramids, men in kaffiyehs, exotic women, and onion-domed mosques remain as central components of a stereotypical scene. This usually implies latent or actual violence directed outward at "unbelievers" or inward toward women. As many Muslim women who wear head scarves in public have attested, non-Muslim Westerners often assume that they cover themselves under the coercive command of their fathers or husbands, whereas many—though certainly not all—have chosen to do so over the protests of these men.[6] Despite nearly one and a half thousand years of Jewish-Christian-Muslim interaction and dialogue, most Western Jews and Christians today are likely to depict Muslims as holding military jihad ("holy struggle") as a central tenet, although only a small minority of Muslims today and historically has ever engaged in religiously motivated armed conflict. The 2005 riots that overtook many French cities demonstrated the presumption of this violent tendency. Although led by some North African immigrants and their French-born children who felt racially marginalized as Arabs and roundly rejected as French, the riots were depicted promptly by many newscasters as instigated by Muslims. No evidence existed that they acted out of religious motivations. The assumption behind this conclusion expects any violence perpetuated by someone who happens to be Muslim to be religious by nature. This only deepens Islamophobia among non-Muslim Westerners.

Islamophobia: "anxiety of Islam"? Can this really be compared to individual psychological traumas such as acrophobia, arachnophobia, or xenophobia? The authors believe that "Islamophobia" accurately reflects a *social* anxiety toward Islam and Muslim cultures that is largely unexamined by, yet deeply ingrained in, Americans. Instead of arising from traumatic personal experiences, like its more psychological cousins, this phobia results for most from distant social experiences that mainstream American culture has perpetuated in popular memory, which are in turn buttressed by a similar understanding of current events. This anxiety relies on a sense of otherness, despite many common sources of thought. So, for example, the shared centrality of ancient Greek thought in European and Arab philosophy seldom finds notice in popular publications. Nor do these sources commonly mention the mutual influence on one another of Judaic, Christian, and Islamic theologies. Meanwhile, the concerns of Muslims—whether they live in Damascus, Delhi, or Detroit—regarding their children's exposure to Hollywood violence or their loss of jobs to an increasingly globalized market do not differ substantially from those of non-Muslim Americans.

Unfortunately, American and European attention has focused most readily on divergence instead of convergence. For example, we might consider the geographic proximity of the roots claimed by mainstream America and Muslims. Until the recent challenges of multiculturalism, the custodians of American culture traced the historical trajectory of that culture backward along an arc reaching through Europe to the ancient eastern Mediterranean: Rome, Greece, and Egypt. Often overlooked is the fact that the Arabs of the medieval period bear primary responsibility for bequeathing the Greek classics to "the West" as it emerged from its self-described "Dark Ages," having translated and developed them in Arabic over centuries. Religiously, too, American popular wisdom has alienated itself from Islam as it has defined Christianity and Judaism as "Western religious traditions" and Islam as an "Eastern religious tradition." This is so despite the fact that the first two religions originated in a region less than two hundred miles west of Islam's historical birthplace, and that the three religions share a mutual heritage of monotheism.

Of course, most Americans seldom think about Muslims or Islam since they are unlikely to encounter either. With only 6 million Muslims in a population of 300 million and little representation on film or television (beyond the news), the public profile of most American Muslims remains low. Meanwhile, beyond Jerusalem, Egypt, and Delhi, places with significant Muslim populations have rarely featured prominently on American tourist itineraries. However, in times of crisis, such as the Iranian hostage situation or, most recently, the September 11 attacks, long-simmering resentments, suspicions, and fears manifest themselves most directly in conditions that appear to affirm many Americans' darkest concerns.

The importance of recognizing these sentiments grows increasingly more urgent for three reasons. First, foreign Muslim populations increasingly consider expanding American interests as antithetical to their own and American foreign policy as threatening to Muslim-majority states. Second, as a tiny but dedicated fraction of these populations employ very lethal means of retaliating against what they perceive as the anti-Islamic or anti-Muslim policies of the United States government, these sentiments will appear to be confirmed among Americans. Third, as increasing numbers of Muslims live in the United States—and will soon represent the largest non-Christian religious population—they increasingly become the targets of hate crimes and discrimination, particularly after attacks by international Muslim militants with whom only the smallest numbers of American Muslims have any sympathy.

Like a vicious cyclone feeding off of its own energy, these sentiments cumulatively feed policies that in turn produce reactions that reinforce the original sentiments. Certainly, American suspicions of Muslims and their rage regarding the attacks of September 11 eased popular acceptance of the Bush administration's claims that Saddam Hussein's

Iraq had cultivated ties with Islamic terrorists and harbored weapons of mass destruction that they might pass to radical Islamic organizations or rogue Muslim governments. For some Americans, domestic Muslims either have come under increasing suspicion as a potential fifth column or have become symbols of "those people." Meanwhile, in the aftermath of the invasion of Iraq, Muslim opinion of the United States in most countries has plummeted. Despite the assurances of the administration that their war targets terrorism—not Islam—its use of the term "crusade," its invasion of two Muslim-majority countries and belligerence toward Iran and Syria, and the employment of Christian aid organizations in reconstruction efforts all appear to reaffirm international and domestic Muslim opinion that Americans inherently distrust and disrespect Muslims. The outrage this prompts among many Muslims feeds violent responses perpetrated by a few, which, completing the cycle, are used to justify yet more attacks against Muslim targets.

The present work attempts to demonstrate the presence of these anxieties by examining one particular type of popular expression: the political cartoon. Whereas previous authors have documented very clearly the anti-Muslim content of literature, film, and the media in general,[7] none have considered political cartoons at length. These cartoons offer vivid expressions of Islamophobia because they are images created as immediate responses to events. As such, they clearly express the latent sensibilities of their cartoonists (and, by extension, of society), who must craft their responses quickly in order to remain current. Whereas verbal expressions are subordinated more easily to the internalized editor of cultural sensitivity, the visual borrows from a broad pool of images and symbols that have largely escaped criticism. Our argument is not that these depictions represent prejudiced artists, but that they reflect widely disseminated attitudes among non-Muslim Americans, including the artists.

This term "Islamophobia" hopes to suggest just this latency. Its invisible normality makes the antagonism toward Islam and Muslims that is inherent in so much of American mainstream culture difficult to engage, let alone counter. This remains particularly evident in the editorial choices of broadcasters and newspapers. Since the September 11 attacks, it has become common to hear media figures and everyday folk argue with statements that most Muslims do not support that crime and similar acts of violence. They ask, "Where are the moderate Muslims? If most Muslims don't like the terrorists, why don't their leaders say so?" When asked, "How would you know if they did condemn the violence?" they reply, with absolute confidence, that their news sources would certainly tell them.

Sadly, media outlets consistently overlook the voices of moderation that come from the majority of Muslims. When violence flared in 2006 over the controversial Danish cartoons of the Prophet Muhammad, most of America's frontline newspapers took days to report—if they did at all—the condemnation of the violence issued immediately by the Council on American-Islamic Relations (CAIR), one of the most important Islamic organizations in the United States and only one of many that decried the attacks. In another instance the year before, a Connecticut newspaper ran an editorial decrying the lack of public statements by Muslim leaders against the then-recent terrorist attacks in London.[8] The state chapter of CAIR wrote back asking why the newspaper had not mentioned its own denunciation of the violence, which the group had sent the newspaper. In fact, since this event, a great variety and number of Muslim leaders in the United States and abroad condemned the attacks but received little coverage by the American media. A large proportion of Americans rely on the mass media for news of the world, but this collection of news and entertainment agencies operates under most of the same ingrained perspectives as their audiences. Their reporting reinforces these views, challenging them only at the risk of losing popularity, ratings, and commercial success. Political cartoons also reflect many of these perspectives as they too are edited and selected by the same system.

Some might protest that cartoons are not a very appropriate medium by which to examine American perspectives and sentiments. They are, after all, "only joking." But the prevalence of editorial cartoons in newspapers, news magazines, and online news sites demonstrates how popular—and effective—they are. William "Boss" Tweed, the infamous New York City politician of the nineteenth century, once said of the cartoons Thomas Nast drew to criticize him, "Stop them damn pictures. I don't care so much what the papers write about me. My constituents can't read. But, damn it, they can see pictures."[9] He was not alone in his appraisal of the damage Nast's cartoons did. Ulysses S. Grant attributed "the sword of Sheridan and the pencil of Thomas Nast" for his successful presidential campaign of 1868.[10] Even the near-total absence of cartoons of any sort in the print edition in the *New York Times* perhaps testifies to the power of the political cartoon. One *Times* editor recently remarked, "Cartoons suck the air out of editorial pages because they are the one thing many people glom onto. In other words, they get in the way of people reading the page more closely."[11]

Editorial cartoons are popular for some very clear reasons. Among these is their ability to communicate in a very brief but powerful fashion ideas and sentiments resonant with readers. Through the use of humor in particular, editorial cartoons may speak the unspoken, explicitly connecting with implicit assumptions of their readers in ways that generate powerful responses: readers nod their heads in avid agreement, shake their heads in grim acknowledgment, and cut out their favorites to share with friends or hang on refrigerator doors and office walls. Cartoons often capture not only contemporary thoughts but feelings regarding current events: the rage regarding Pearl Harbor, the sorrow of John F. Kennedy's assassination, the frustration of Vietnam, the devastation of 9/11. Many cartoonists clearly consider themselves to be protective critics for American society. For instance, cartoonist Walt Kelly understood the function of the political cartoonist to be "that of the watchdog. It is the duty of the watchdog to growl warnings, to bark, to surmise that every strange footfall is that of a cat."[12]

This work does not attempt to detail the causes of the antagonisms and conflicts to which it refers through the cartoons. This is not a matter of blaming Americans or Westerners for the current controversies. Undoubtedly, some Muslims use equally simplistic and bias-laden images in their depictions of Americans. For instance, concern has been raised regarding occasionally racist depictions of Jews in Middle Eastern cartoons. However, the incredible power—economic, political, cultural, and military—that the United States projects throughout the world today demands that Americans accept the responsibility to understand and engage the people beyond (and increasingly within) its borders with the least historical impairment possible.

Many, if not most, Americans have little appreciation for the daily impact American lifestyles and values have on the world. It is not, after all, Americans who flock to mushrooming numbers of foreign fast-food restaurants, or Americans who worry about the foreign values instilled in their children by pervasive and eye-catching foreign films and music channels, or Americans who worry about the impact on their population and politics of foreign military personnel stationed in their country. This imparts to Americans a greater responsibility to question the norms by which they understand themselves and the world, not in order to reject their systems of values out of hand, but to put them in perspective relative to those of others who will be far less interested in exploring those values if they suspect an inherent lack of respect toward their own.

There are those who have responded with wrath to similar arguments for American responsibility. They judge such comments to be "anti-American" because they imply blame on the victims (Americans) and justification for the victimizers (Muslims). We believe that the virulence of these responses reflects the degree to which certain views described in this book have been normalized. That is, they demonstrate *how natural* for so many Americans *the image* of Muslims as irrational aggressors and Americans as righteous innocents abroad and at home (and the mutual exclusion of these two groups) has become, so that any other perspective becomes not a counterargument but a challenge to an unquestionable world order. The emotional outrage that such views at times elicit reflects the deep investment many Americans have in a self-perception of their nation as a force of goodness in a world defined by either evil or capitulation.

Because Muslims seldom appear in news reports or other media sources except as perpetrators of violence, supposedly in the name of Islam, many Americans understandably conclude that all Muslims act from inherently religious motivations, and that Islam is dangerous. Muslims become two-dimensional, existing only *as Muslims*, seemingly never sharing identities or interests with non-Muslims. However, non-Muslim Americans engage Muslim Americans in thousands of ways every day: a student and her classmates, a banker and his customer, a police officer and a family in need of help, a homeowner and her neighbors. Moreover, Americans and foreign Muslims encounter one another daily in hundreds of thousands of interactions. The globalized world we inhabit makes possible increasingly intimate connections between distant individuals with increasing speed. Why, despite all of this contact, do domestic news and entertainment sources seldom mention the terms "Muslim" or "Islam" except in the context of conflict, violence, and bloodshed?

Our argument here is not that the American or Western depiction of Muslims and Islam has not changed for the past fourteen hundred years, or even the past forty. However, what has remained constant has been a nervousness and distrust of those associated with these terms, a persistent sense that to be Muslim is to be a distrusted Other. The exact terms of that otherness depend on the self-understanding of those doing the imagining. Meanwhile, as the recent controversy about the Danish cartoons has amply shown, the accelerating pace of globalization, transportation, and communication has meant that the expressions of these perceptions travel to an increasingly farther and wider audience that can, with increasing impact, respond in diverse ways. Hollywood films project popular American representations of Muslims in movie theaters and on home televisions in myriad cities around the globe. Foreign journalists report the latest American government policy toward Iran or the Palestinians through simultaneous international broadcasts. Meanwhile, the Internet allows people throughout the world to read American newspapers, including their political cartoons.

It has been observed that movements against discrimination do not begin until a commonly understood label evolves that brings together under one banner all forms of that particular prejudice. Resistance to gender discrimination coalesced around the term "sexism." The civil rights movement gained momentum when harnessed to the notion of "racism" that encapsulated the variety of innate prejudices and institutional obstacles in a white-dominated society. The concept of "anti-Semitism" has provided a powerful tool to object to anti-Jewish sentiment that was once, like the denigrations of women and blacks, considered normal and left largely unchallenged by people fitting the norm. Increasingly, and particularly among Muslims, "Islamophobia" provides a term to similarly draw attention to a normalized prejudice and unjustified discrimination. Undoubtedly this term will elicit the same unease among and even backlash from some of those whose notions of normal it challenges, just as its historical predecessors have and still do.

• 1 •

Overview of Western
Encounters with Muslims

During the first half of 2003, Gen. William G. Boykin, deputy undersecretary of defense for intelligence, addressed a series of Christian groups. Reflecting on his experience in Somalia as American military forces battled against the fractious warlords of that starvation-threatened country, especially the elusive and powerful Mohammad Farrah Aidid, General Boykin offered comparisons meant to explicitly define the distinctive qualities of the United States. At the time, the nation struggled with the repercussions of September 11, celebrated the demise of the Taliban in Afghanistan, and geared up for an invasion of Iraq. And so, in June 2003, he addressed the First Baptist Church of Broken Arrow, Oklahoma, and asked:

> But who is that enemy? It's not Osama bin Laden. Our enemy is a spiritual enemy because we are a nation of believers. You go back and look at our history, and you will find that we were founded on faith. Look at what the writers of the Constitution said. We are a nation of believers. We were founded on faith. And the enemy that has come against our nation is a spiritual enemy. His name is Satan. And if you do not believe that Satan is real, you are ignoring the same Bible that tells you about God. Now I'm a warrior. One day I'm going to take off this uniform and I'm still going to be a warrior. And what I'm here to do today is to recruit you to be warriors of God's kingdom.

Earlier in the year, Boykin had offered a very specific example of the manifest power of God in America's affairs when he addressed the First Baptist Church in Dayton, Florida. He reflected on Osman Atto, a

Somali leader who became an American target and narrowly missed capture:

> And then he went on CNN and he laughed at us, and he said, "They'll never get me because Allah will protect me. Allah will protect me."
>
> Well, you know what? I knew that my God was bigger than his. I knew that my God was a real God, and his was an idol. But I prayed, Lord let us get that man.
>
> Three days later we went after him again, and this time we got him. Not a mark on him. We got him. We brought him back into our base there and we had a Sea Land container set up to hold prisoners in, and I said put him in there. They put him in there, there was one guard with him. I said search him, they searched him, and then I walked in with no one in there but the guard, and I looked at him and said, "Are you Osman Atto?" And he said, "Yes." And I said, "Mr. Atto, you underestimated our God."[1]

When a video of these addresses came to the attention of newspapers and television news programs, a debate erupted. Because Boykin wore his uniform while making these remarks, various American political and religious figures argued that he should be reprimanded for making divisive comments while dressed as a representative of the United States armed forces. Despite the protests, no such reprimand has been forthcoming.[2]

Boykin's perspective and the complaints against it reflect the twin roots of Islamophobia in the United States. On the one hand, many Christians undoubtedly applaud Boykin's unfettered public expression of their own sentiments that God actively stirs America's destiny to counter evil—as personified by Satan—and to correct the idolatrous like Osman Atto. For them, the world is divided between those on the side of the angels and those who oppose them. Those in the middle are complicit with evil or otherwise compromised. Proponents of this view unwittingly lay claim to a theological heritage that, since the earliest days of Islam, considers Muslims as inherently dangerous because of their (at best) erroneous understandings or (at worst) satanic strivings.

On the other hand, many Americans interpret the stridency of Boykin's statements and their potential negative impact as a demonstration of the threat religion presents when expressed in public or by public officials (in this case a military official in uniform who holds a public position). Indeed, some of these individuals may consider themselves devoutly Christian or otherwise religious, yet they remain suspicious of those who promote, practice, or espouse their religion outside the privacy of their homes and places of worship. Informed by the tenacious Western idea that Islam persistently, even fanatically, strives for dominion over all dimensions of life—particularly the political—many Americans remain inherently wary of Muslims. Although many Americans may suspect politically committed Christians some of the time, they doubt most Muslims most of the time.

The brief historical overview that follows mentions the turning point when many Europeans changed their characterization of Muslims from a competitor in theology according to Christian doctrine to an abiding religious threat according to a secularist worldview. Key to this shift in perception was the emergence of secularism in the eighteenth century. Although most Europeans defined themselves and their societies as Christians before this, secular ideals increasingly valued national over religious identity. As we shall see, this meant that as Europeans shifted the understanding of their social order from one identified primarily as Christian to one known principally as secular, "Muslim" continued to serve as a negative identity by which first Christian and then secular norms could be contrasted, defined, and valorized. Distinctively, American mainstream culture projects this expectation of a secular social order while in other ways reinforcing the characterization of the United States as divinely mandated and guided as, indeed, "one nation, under God."

Although an amazing array of influences shapes American popular culture and the population collectively counts every country as a source of ethnic heritage, there can be no denying that Europe and its forms of Christianity loom largest on the American cultural landscape. This is so because some European Christians and their descendants held—and still hold (though less absolutely)—the greatest economic and political power, and so exerted the greatest influence in defining the nascent nation. Although a large number of the earliest Americans did not count Europe as their place of origin (specifically the millions of Native Americans and enslaved Africans), their relative lack of influence by and large left their unique perspectives out of the equation. Nevertheless, their descendants often became thoroughly imbued with the European cultural inheritance that seemed so normal to European Americans through the reinforcement of public education and the mass media. The following account, therefore, traces the passage of Islamophobia to the United States through Europe as a general cultural inheritance even as it recognizes that an increasingly smaller proportion of Americans lay claim to Europe in their personal heritage.

Because of its brevity, this historical outline is necessarily incomplete and fails to describe many of the nuanced changes that occurred over time. It focuses instead on the most significant and pervasive themes that have persisted throughout these fourteen hundred years: religiously tinged anxiety regarding Muslims, theological depreciation of Islam, and a grudging respect for Arab Muslims. This reluctant regard evolved out of specific moments in the relationship between Europe and Muslims: the success in equal combat of Arab Muslim armies and the remarkable emblems of diverse Muslim civilizations. However, these positive impressions seemed to always occur as but lingering moments in some battle for supremacy that, finally, only reaffirmed anxieties and fears that have loomed larger than positive impressions since the beginning of Islam.

In keeping with the overall theme of the book, this chapter restricts most of its discussion to non-Muslim Western perspectives on Muslims and Islam. Of course, Muslims have had their own perspectives on interrelations. A general history of the mutual engagements, interactions, interpenetrations, and antagonisms would require more attention to Muslim views, but since the present work engages in an already different task, we can only refer readers interested in these important perspectives to the works listed on this topic in the bibliography.

THE SPREAD OF ISLAM AND COMPETITION WITH CHRISTIANITY

In 610 CE, a man by the name of Muhammad declared that he had begun to receive revelations from the god, Allah ("the One"), who he considered to be the one and only god. Although some in Mecca, the Arab city in which he lived, welcomed him as a prophet, others felt threatened theologically and economically by this critic of a social order in many ways reliant on the pilgrimage of nomadic tribes to Mecca to visit the images of their various deities installed there. Devotees housed many of these images in a large, cubical structure called the Kaba, which Muslims believed to be an ancient mosque, the first place constructed to worship Allah. Forced by mounting oppression to leave Mecca but guided by the continuing revelations, the early community of Muslims departed Mecca in 622 and settled in Medina, a city whose leaders had invited Muhammad to act as arbitrator of their urban squabbles. These followers called themselves "Muslims," the Arabic word for "one who submits," which is related to the word "Islam," meaning "submission." These words occurred in the revelations that referred to themselves collectively as both "the book" and "the recitation" (Quran). Muhammad made the conversion of the residents of Medina, excepting its Jewish tribes, a precondition of his move there.

Recognizing Muhammad as not only a prophet but also a leader of this, the first Islamic society, Muslims in Medina agreed to live according to the many guidelines and rules revealed to Muhammad in an effort to engender a new ideal of social justice and divine relationship. As a social leader, Muhammad became distinct from foundational figures associated with certain other religions, such as Jesus and the Buddha, because he did not live as an itinerant teacher focused primarily on preaching. Instead, like David, Solomon, Rama, Ashoka, Constantine, and other religious exemplars of leadership, Muhammad became head of state and took on associated duties. These included leading military operations when necessary.

Armed defense became a paramount concern for the next decade as Meccan leaders became incensed with the Muslims for another economic reason. The Medinian Muslims, following traditions long common among Arabs, raided trade caravans. These caravans represented the economic foundation of Meccan merchants who mounted military expeditions to assault the Muslim raiders and their city. The many routs Muslims achieved in battle served as signs of Allah's support for their cause. Meanwhile, the need for defense of the Muslim community became legitimized through the concept of jihad, or striving. Indeed, it is written in the Quran, "Fight those in the way of God who fight you, but do not be aggressive: God does not like aggressors" (2.190). Meanwhile, the Prophet put armed jihad in perspective when a returning warrior extolled Muslim victories. The Prophet replied that two types of jihad existed: the lesser was the struggle against the enemies of Islam and the greater was against the evil within oneself. Ultimately, Muhammad's success in military leadership and diplomatic finesse led to the nearly bloodless capitulation of Mecca and the rededication of the Kaba to Allah alone.

Muhammad's diplomacy not only allowed for the union of the disparate tribes on the Arabian Peninsula during his lifetime but also made possible the astonishing expansion of this united Arab power following his death. Perhaps propelled by a population that had begun burgeoning before the advent of Islam, Arab armies unified by an Islamic ideology quickly moved out of the peninsula and, within but one hundred years, fashioned an empire that stretched from the Iberian Peninsula of contemporary Spain and Portugal to the western edge of what is today Pakistan. This success came at the particular expense of the Byzantine Empire. With its capital in Constantinople, the Byzantines had dominated the Mediterranean Sea for centuries. They understood themselves to be the orthodox successor to both the Roman Empire and the Christian Church. Their emperors legitimated their rule through the Orthodox Christianity that they lavishly sponsored. The singular success of Muslim Arabs to displace both Byzantine rule and Orthodox dominance in such stalwart Christian realms as North Africa shocked the rulers and prelates alike and challenged their expectations for the success of Christendom. Christians had understood the astonishing growth of their movement from diminutive Jewish sect to Roman persecuted church to official imperial religion as evidence of the miracle of Christ's Word and the inexorable Christian spirit. The sudden loss of so much Byzantine territory and accelerating conversions of Christian souls precipitated three responses common in most cases of competition: (1) an effort to explain the losses and (2) an attempt to disparage the competitor while (3) affirming the truth of the home team. (Not all Christians felt this way. Those communities outside the fold of the dominant form of Christianity, such as the Copts of Egypt, often welcomed Muslim rule. Because of their recognition of Christians as recipients of early instances of Allah's revelation, Muslim rulers often afforded protection to minority Christian groups against the persecution they regularly experienced under Roman Catholic and Orthodox rule. Jews, too, often benefited from Muslim rule because of their recognition as "People of the Book," hence Muhammad's exemption from conversion of the Jewish tribes of Medina.)

For many, if the success of Christianity and the expansion of Christendom resulted from the grace of God, then the success of Islam and the expansion of Muslim rule must be either the outcome of grace or the result of some other supernatural force. Obviously, since the former conclusion necessarily displaced Christianity as God's Truth, most Christians were unlikely to embrace it. In the binary world of medieval Christianity—where God stood countered by Satan, good by evil—the alternative meant that Satan must have engendered these successes. Jews had already, at times, been depicted within this framework as handmaidens of Satan and a community blinded by deceit. A similar place would be added for Muslims.

Christians often also responded through efforts to disparage their competitors. Although there was no centrally planned program of disinformation, the disparagement commonly focused on three elements of Islam: the person of Muhammad, the message of the Quran, and the character of Muslim societies. While Christian writers certainly chose a topic sensitive for Muslims when they condemned Muhammad, they did so with a misperception of his role for most Muslims. It is true that no person has as much stature for most Muslims as Muhammad. As recipient of the final revelation of God, as leader of the first Muslim community, and as the exemplar of Muslim behavior, Muhammad continues to hold a very special place of veneration among Muslims. However, Christians often assumed his role in Islam to be comparable to that of Christ in Christianity. The parallel is a faulty one. The thrust for Muslims, as is obvious from the story of the purging of the images of the various gods and goddesses in the Kaba, is that Allah alone should be worshipped, never a human.[3] When Muhammad died in 634, one of his closest followers immediately declared, "O men, if anyone worships Muhammad, Muhammad is dead: if anyone worships God, God is alive, immortal."[4] Although many Europeans and some Muslims would refer to Muslims as "Muhammadans," most Muslims now bristle at the term because their faith and practice centers on Allah, not Muhammad.

Nevertheless, Muhammad became the target of Christian derision. Attacks often focused on one or both of two features: Muhammad as a hedonist and Muhammad as a shyster. The contrast appeared stark when comparing Jesus' presumed sexual chastity, material impoverishment, political disinterest, and devotion to peace with Muhammad's multiple marriages, economic involvement, political rule, and military leadership. For instance, Muhammad's marriage to fourteen wives contrasts starkly with Jesus' celibacy. Since Jesus provided the paradigm of godliness for Christians, Muhammad seemed to be his polar opposite. Muslims, as evidenced by their deep regard for Muhammad and his message, indicted themselves as similarly hedonistic and misdirected. In an odd paradox that will be better understood when we consider the issue of "norm" in chapter 3, later Europeans and Americans would criticize Muhammad for his perceived puritanical stringency as evidenced by restrictions on the consumption of wine and the segregation of men and women.

Anyone who has read the Quran will know that the derision has flowed both ways. Passages in the Quran warn against the faulty conclusions of Christians that Jesus, an important prophet for Muslims, existed as the incarnation of God. In fact, various lines in the Quran repeat the claim that it provides a perfect replacement for the preceding books, as described below.

Such supposed misdirection of Muslims, and of many converted Christians, demonstrated the other Christian accusation against Muhammad: that he scammed his followers. For this reason, Dante consigned the Prophet, and his son-in-law Ali, to the second-lowest circle of hell in his *Inferno* (even as he borrowed, perhaps unconsciously, the notion of nine levels of heaven and hell from Islamic theology!):[5]

> A rundlet [cask], that hath lost
> Its middle or side stave, gaps not so wide
> As one I marked, torn from the chin throughout
> Down to the hinder passage: 'twixt the legs
> Dangling his entrails hung, the midriff lay
> Open to view, and wretched ventricle,
> That turns the englutted [swallowed] aliment to dross [excrement].
> Whilst eagerly I fix on him my gaze,
> He eyed me, with his hands laid his breast bare,
> And cried, "Now mark how I do rip me: lo!
> How is Mohammed mangled: before me
> Walks Ali weeping, from the chin his face
> Cleft to the forelock; and the others all,
> Whom here thou seest, while they lived, did sow
> Scandal and schism, and therefore thus are rent . . ."[6]

Nowhere could this charge of scam artist be better demonstrated than in the "heresy" of the book that Muhammad championed as a correction of the Christian Bible.

If the analogy between Christ and Muhammad fails because Christians understand Christ as God incarnate and Muslims accept Muhammad as only human, then the more correct analogy would be between Christ and the Quran. The followers of each religion understand both the Messiah and the Book to be the physical expression of God's word.[7] Although Muslims revere Muhammad for many reasons, none surpasses his role as the medium through which the final revelation came to humanity. The Quran claims itself to be the answer to previous failures on the part of humans to maintain free from error God's earlier efforts to send books of guidance to three specially chosen prophets. As such it surpasses the Psalms sent to David, the Torah sent to Moses, and the Gospels sent to Jesus. Thus, the Quran refers to Jews and Christians as "People of the Book" who had previously received written revelation, as opposed to kafir ("unbelievers") who never had. If the medieval churches condemned Jews for failing to recognize the truth of the "New" Testament and remaining mired in the legalism of the "Old" Testament, then this Muslim claim of a correction to both would obviously not be well received. The Quran was roundly attacked as a spuriously written book concocted by the devious Muhammad for his own material and political gain and/or because of his manipulation by Satan.

All these responses intended to reaffirm the truth of Christianity and the institutions that perpetuated its practice and teachings. By negating the purported claims of Islam, it was hoped that Christianity would be affirmed inherently. Nevertheless, even in the Middle Ages there existed those who considered the similarities between Judaism, Christianity, and Islam as favorably comparable and cause for communication. Pope Gregory VII, in a letter to a Muslim Algerian prince, wrote, "[T]here is a charity which we owe to each other more than to other peoples because we recognize and confess one sole God, although in different ways, and we praise and worship Him every day as creator and ruler of the world." Although he probably had political reasons to highlight this common ground and would write harshly about Muslims elsewhere, this pope's conceptualization of any common ground remains significant, if not widely embraced by Christians.[8]

THE CRUSADES

No event would appear to be more emblematic of the seemingly inevitable conflict between Christians and Muslims than the Crusades. The use of the term today by Muslim extremists to condemn any Western presence in the Middle East appears to confirm their commitment to viewing the world through a religious lens. However, it is significant that the Crusaders unintentionally ignited an Islamic unity that had previously not existed in the region since the waning of the original Islamic empire established immediately following Muhammad's death. It was the Christian ideology of conquest that inspired an equally effective—and ultimately more successful—Islamic ideology of defense. Meanwhile Europeans and Middle Easterners were mutually impressed by the courage and ability of one another in the ferocity of combat.

The Crusades provided one of the salient memories for both European Christians and eastern Mediterranean Muslims of their interactions. Although most Americans consider themselves too future-oriented and pragmatic to be mired in the enduring antagonisms and balkanizing strife of the "old world" of Europe or the Middle East, very old social memories nevertheless resonate in popular American culture. They do so on an almost unconscious level that remains unnoticed by most people in their everyday lives. One need only reflect on the prevalence of the term "crusader" in popular culture to see this point. Many school teams, social activists, and community leaders proudly refer to themselves as crusaders and may indeed adopt the anachronistic image of the armor-clad knight with jousting pole and cross-emblazoned shield mounted upon a brawny steed as their mascot or emblem. The American military certainly embraced this image when they named an important North African campaign in World War II Operation Crusader,[9] supplied the Navy with the F-8 Crusader fighter aircraft beginning in the 1950s, and almost financed the state-of-the-art Crusader self-propelled gun in the 1990s. And if the pervasiveness of the symbol does not seem evidence enough of the potency of the memory, one only need consider the widespread memory of Richard the Lionheart recognized by many, if not most, Americans, for no other reason that his presence as the well-meaning English hero in most renditions of the Robin Hood legend. He appears as an indispensable component of film portrayals from Douglas Fairbanks's 1922 classic to Kevin Costner's *Prince of Thieves*.

The Crusades, however, did not begin with Richard the Lionheart but with the head of the Roman Catholic Church, Pope Urban II. Recognizing an opportunity to expand the influence of the Church abroad and tapping into a pool of unengaged European noble youths who both lacked opportunities to exercise their ambitions and sought penitential acts to ameliorate their sins,[10] the pope suggested that an assault should be mounted to free Jerusalem from Muslim rule. Jerusalem had long been a destination for Christian pilgrims who sought to visit the places associated with Jesus' final days, crucifixion, and resurrection. At times, brigands (many of whom were Muslim but acted out of greed, not religious animosity) robbed these pilgrims. By identifying these bandits primarily as Muslims, the pope successfully fired a *religious* enthusiasm for his effort. Urban II, in his written call for a crusade, encouraged Christians to hasten to the aid of the Byzantine Empire, "your brethren in the east," which had lost lands to "the Turks and the Arabs." Synonyms Urban used in his letter for the latter groups included "vile race," "pagans," "infidels," "barbarians," and "a despised and base race, which worships demons." These descriptions contrasted with references to those who would heed his call as "sons of God," "the faithful of God," "Christ's heralds," and those with "the faith of omnipotent God."[11] This antagonism toward not only Muslims but non–Christians in general proved such a successful motivator that the First Crusade began with assaults on various Jewish communities in Europe itself resulting in slaughters, like those in Mainz and Worms that murdered almost all resident Jews.[12] When this army appeared at the walls of Constantinople, the capital of the Byzantine Empire, the emperor there welcomed them with trepidation, not knowing whether their antagonism would extend to the Orthodox Christians under his rule.

Although some authors might depict this as only the first of a series of unavoidable conflicts between implacable foes, this was not the case. The popular assumption that the Crusades comprised a battle between Christianity and Islam assumes that both sides understood themselves primarily through a religious lens. In fact, the initial success of the Crusades was made possible just as much by the collective response of European Christians to the pope's call as by the very lack of a unifying ideology or identity among those in eastern Mediterranean countries who found themselves under attack. Although most of the rulers of the diverse kingdoms in that region were Muslims, they were as likely at war with one another as with Christians, as was the case among Christian princes in Europe. Political power and economic wealth motivated conflict far more than religious identity did. Ironically, the Crusaders' violent antagonism toward Muslims and their example of a successfully unifying religious identity inspired the Kurdish general Salah ud-Din (anglicized as "Saladin") to use Islam to promote a unified defense. It worked. Jerusalem soon fell to Salah ud-Din and the Crusaders slowly retreated in defeat, although the region would be convulsed by crusading efforts for the next two centuries. North Africa and the Balkans would be objects of crusades until the sixteenth and seventeenth centuries, respectively.[13]

And so, although before the Crusaders' arrival the Middle East had been a group of disparate kingdoms that happened to have Muslim rulers, after their departure these kingdoms became a set of larger, more powerful states operating more centrally—if not consistently—from Islamic ideologies. Reflecting the growth of the movement to include attacks on any non-Latin Christian community for political purposes, the later Crusaders sacked the previously unvanquished city of Constantinople in 1204 in a naked exercise of political expansion. Ironically, this perhaps contributed to the capture of the weakened city in 1453 by the Turks who had long sought its submission. The newly renamed Istanbul would serve as the capital of the Ottoman Empire for the next four centuries. Meanwhile, the ascent of the sophisticated Ottomans, who would control Greece and the Balkans, advancing as far as Vienna, provided a new sense of Muslim threat to the rest of Europe.

Nevertheless, the Crusaders' experience in the eastern Mediterranean, although fired by a depreciative theological perspective, often allowed for a respect for some "Saracens," their term for Arab Muslims (deriving, perhaps, from the Arabic *sharqi*, "eastern"). European folklore would describe the magnanimous heroism of Saladin and his personal relationship with Richard the Lionheart based upon their mutual respect for one another's bravery and chivalry. Favorable Western representations of Saladin can be seen even as recently as Hollywood's Crusade epic *The Kingdom of Heaven* (2005). The fear of the scimitar that inspired European Christians to take it as a symbol of Islam and fanaticism also compelled a respect for the technological sophistication of certain Arab swords. The scimitar as a European symbol of Islam, then, reflects the double-edged quality of many European attitudes toward Muslims: the same warfare skills, civilizational successes, and religious devotion that engendered such anxieties also encouraged some respect. Perhaps for this reason the British have named their army's latest assault vehicle "Scimitar," a successor to the armored car "Saladin" and armored personnel carrier "Saracen" deployed a few decades after they fielded their "Crusader" tank in World War II. However, this respect arises only in the larger context of Christian European antipathy for Muslims as inherently warlike,

Muslim civilizations as manifestly decadent, and Islamic theology as decidedly heretical.

THE RECONQUISTA

This pattern of using a Christian ideology to unite a group in the pursuit of economic and political expansion would be repeated at the other end of the Mediterranean Sea. Since the Arab conquests in the eighth century, Jews, Christians, and Muslims cooperated in an amazing common culture that had evolved on the Iberian Peninsula. Benefiting from the transmission of the Greek classics through Arabic writers, the lands of present-day Spain and Portugal enjoyed an intellectual and artistic flourishing that allowed for, and owed equally to, the Jewish philosopher Maimonides and the Muslim philosopher ibn Sina (Avicenna), whose medical texts would be used in European medical colleges for centuries. Although described as "Muslim Spain," the actual tenets of Islam had little to do with political governing and decision making on the Iberian Peninsula until at least 1000 CE.[14] Clearly, there was no contrast between "the West" and "the Muslim world" here. Nevertheless, ambitious Christian political leaders later sharpened a diatribe against the "Moor" (or Iberian Muslim).[15]

Although northern kingdoms had sought expansion into the Muslim-dominated south for centuries, they had not used religious motivation to unite a common Christian opposition to the Moors. Alliances fluidly shifted so that Christians and Muslims would be as likely to be allied with fellow Christians and Muslims as in opposition to them.[16] However, at the same time he launched the First Crusade against Palestine, Pope Urban II also encouraged a crusade in Iberia. The northern kingdoms soon realized the power that a crusading ideology lent to their political efforts and enjoined their nobles and peasants to join in the united Christian campaign against Muslims. This effectively polarized all parts of the political contest into two sides and forced Arabs to view themselves as Muslims qua Muslims, engaged in the defense of Islamic territory. But the ideology of a unified Christendom could not easily overcome the political suspicions and rivalries between the self-described Christian kingdoms, and so the Reconquista dragged on for centuries. The final assault against the last "Moorish" state, Grenada, succeeded in large part due to the financial backing of successive popes[17] for the courts of Castile and Aragon. Allied through the marriage of their rulers, King Ferdinand and Queen Isabella, the armies of these states defeated Grenada in 1492.

Most contemporary Americans associate the year 1492 with at least one of two events: Christopher Columbus's departure on his famous voyage of discovery and the expulsion of the Jews from Spain. These events share more than a common date. It was the economic windfall following Ferdinand and Isabella's final victory that allowed them to finance Columbus's trip. The religious motivation not only made their military success possible, but also led to the expulsion or conversion of all Jews under the threat of execution and inspired Columbus to embark on his perilous voyage in order to find the riches required to militarily liberate Jerusalem.[18] While seldom mentioned in contemporary American accounts of the expulsion of the Iberian Jews, Muslims, too, ultimately suffered the same choice: emigration, conversion, or death.

Although far less well known to popular American audiences, through its victory the Reconquista served to reestablish a supposedly natural Christian order of Europe, just as the Crusades through its defeats affirmed the Arab and Muslim nature of the Middle East. While the Reconquista would be remembered as the closing of a chapter in European history—the term "reconquest" suggesting the restoration of an inherently Christian territory—that enabled the beginning chapter of the "discovery of the New World," the failure of the last crusades permanently cauterized the wound of a lost Jerusalem and established the Middle East as the land of Turks/Arabs/Muslims. This would be reemphasized when Western Europeans returned four centuries later and subjugated these lands to their economic and political—if not military—control with remarkable rapidity.

EUROPEAN IMPERIALISM AND HEGEMONY[19]

The French Revolution and Industrial Revolution notwithstanding, no series of events has had as marked an influence on the modern world than European imperialism and hegemony. The forces of nationalism, capitalism, and industrialization that engendered these other events also served to make possible an astounding projection of power across the globe from the territorially small and demographically insignificant continent of Europe. The wave of exploration that Columbus joined established new lines of transportation that would soon be woven into a global network of communication and exchange by European commercial ventures. Increasingly recognizing the significance of overseas trade and wealth extraction for their economic well-being, European states became increasingly competitive with one another in their quest for new resources for production, new markets for their products, and new ports for their traders and the navies that protected them.

This competition dominated the early colonial history of North America as the Spanish, Dutch, French, and English soon defended their fragile toeholds on the continent with the establishment of more permanent settlements and the aggressive use of military forces. The native inhabitants were often pushed aside or annihilated once their utility—instructing settlers in how to survive in the new climes—was exhausted and they were found not to produce commodities of practical value to Europeans. In a worldview that found significant differentiation only between Christians, Jews, Muslims, and pagans, the indigenous Americans fit into the latter, least respected category and were accorded little concern. Violent efforts by original inhabitants to oust European settlers deepened the antagonism and sharpened the response.

Many of the colonists had left Europe to find respite from the religious persecutions that had washed throughout that continent since the Protestant Reformation. Later Americans would interpret this as emblematic of the unique quality of their country as a haven from religious intolerance. However, this was not, by and large, the case. Few of these previously persecuted groups showed any hesitancy in ridding themselves of those who diverged in dogma or practice from their rigidly defined norms. The Puritans, the exemplary group for this theme, cast out people like Anne Hutchinson, deliberately leaving many to a fate similar to that of her and her family—slaughter outside the protected walls of their theologically defined settlements. Just as surely as groups like the Puritans carried their religious intolerance from Europe into their relations with one another and with the "pagan" natives, they also transported far older antagonisms toward Muslims. Although these, for the most part, did not derive from actual contact, they represented a social memory perpetuated through popular narratives and religious instruction. The responses to the presence of Muslims among African slaves reflect many of the sentiments of the time and are discussed below.

European encounters with Muslims through their expanding imperial projects also served to reinforce antagonisms even as they recharacterized Muslims. This was true in different ways for the variety of European empires that competed with one another's reach across the globe. However, given the space constraints here, we will focus more on the British Empire than others since it had the greatest (but certainly not the only) impact on American impressions.

At its height, the British Empire directly or indirectly controlled one-fifth of the globe's land surface and one-quarter of its people. Such extensive holdings required the British—as it did the other European empires—to subjugate those people who served commercial interests or could not be easily displaced. Due to their recently developed technological sophistication and nationalist social organization, Europeans successfully subordinated other societies on a scale never witnessed before. But this did not amount to a simple military conquest: It would have been impossible for the small European population to control as many non-Europeans as it did through direct coercion. Rather, Europeans maintained their global empires by incorporating local people into their systems of domination. That is, Europeans successfully convinced some conquered people to become agents of their own subjugation. This is a mark of hegemony.

More than simple physical control, hegemony involves the cooperation of the subjugated. This may appear to be willing but must be understood to occur in a situation in which another state or culture controls the context in which the cooperation occurs. So, for instance, almost every person engaged in international business today makes appointments using the Gregorian calendar. Four hundred years ago, at the advent of European imperialism, myriad calendars guided the lives of people around the globe. But the incredible success of the Europeans in dominating other cultures and crafting a system through which most of the world interacts created a global economic and political order that can only be bucked at great cost. Who would decide to use their lunar calendar instead of the solar Gregorian calendar when scheduling an overseas shipment of computers? What would an American bank make of a check written with a date based on the Islamic calendar? The evidence of this hegemonic success can be glimpsed when considering how capitalism has overtaken almost all economies. A global banking system allows an American to withdraw money from her checking account through an ATM in Europe, China, or India. This victory can be seen also in the total eclipse of principalities, cantons, city-states, and the myriad other states that existed even two centuries ago, replaced by some form of the nation-state in which nearly everyone now lives.

But perhaps the most resounding victory for Europeans was not simply that they fashioned the world's economies and political units in their own image, but that they successfully established the means by which many of those they conquered understood themselves. This lent an authority to Europeans in their knowledge not only of the natural world, but of the human realm, too. And so, many institutions—exhibitions, museums, universities, and learned societies—established by Westerners in subjugated lands authoritatively presented information about these domains to those dominated, who increasingly understood themselves using European perspectives. The rising success of Europeans scientifically, economically, militarily, and imperially convinced the conquered to rely on Western ways of knowing the natural and human world.

Of course, many communities and movements resisted European imperialism using violence and other means, but so successful was European hegemony that resistance could be convincingly represented as a rejection of development, not of domination. This was but one of the many ways in which imperialists secured the support of local groups by convincing them of their own inferiority. After all, how to explain their conquest? Many dominated groups accepted the European offer to participate in their own social, political, and economic development and the Western-defined terms through which improvement was described. Those who resisted this vision and the ideals they used to define themselves as apart from European norms came to be negatively defined by Europeans and their allies as "regressive," "traditional," and "backward." Sir Syed Ahmad Khan, a Muslim reformer who founded India's first Western-style college in 1875, defended his efforts against those who feared that Islam would be undermined:

> It is not only because the British are today our rulers, and we have to recognize this fact if we are to survive, that I am advocating the adoption of their system of education, but also because Europe has made such remarkable progress in science that it would be suicidal not to make an effort to acquire it.[20]

Note that Sir Syed self-consciously appreciated the potency of Western science within the context of British domination. For many Europeans, Islam represented such an obstacle to national development. Whereas in the Crusades Europeans saw it as the source of fanatic armed power, now many Westerners would interpret Islam as a force that encouraged insolence, debauchery, and laziness.

This decrepitude among Islamic civilizations seemed particularly prominent in the three previously dominant empires controlled by Muslims: those of the Ottomans in the eastern Mediterranean, the Safavids in Persia (today Iran), and the Mughals in what is now India, Pakistan, and Bangladesh. At a time when Europeans emerged from their Dark Ages, each of these empires had commanded wealth beyond the dreams of any European monarch, patronized towering examples of sophisticated architecture, and controlled huge territories. In an irony of world historical importance, these empires began a period of decline just as Western European empires initiated their ascent. The changing context of competition shifted the terms of the debate and recast Muslims, in part, from fanatic warriors of inexorable conquest to decrepit inheritors of former glories. Cast upon a timeline of world history, Muslims seemed to Europeans as part of a past order surpassed by a new world order defined by them.

Many Europeans justified their imperialism through their efforts to improve and uplift "backward" peoples. These efforts included not only the necessary subjugation of non-Europeans for purposes of ensuring social order but also, at times, proselytism to the true Christian faith. Although among the British, various colonial administrators sought to minimize the presence of missionaries, the rise of a fervent Evangelicalism in the nineteenth century overcame bureaucratic objections in the English Parliament, so missionaries, often with sharply anti-Islamic messages, held forth as never before throughout the British Empire. Reflecting the spirit of competition inherent in much of this thought, one Evangelical-minded British official remarked that Islam was "the only undisguised and formidable antagonist of Christianity . . . an active and powerful enemy. . . . It is just because Muhammadanism acknowledges the divine original, and has borrowed so many of the weapons of Christianity, that it is so dangerous an adversary."[21] The common experience among many missionaries and other proselytizing Evangelicals that Muslims proved particularly resistant to their efforts only deepened their anti-Islamic sentiments.

Imperialists found more success in increasingly reshaping societies in terms of European-style nationalism. As European empires usurped the place of indigenous rulers, they redefined those they conquered as nations: that is, as a unified people of a common character that inhabits a territory defined by internationally recognized borders. To understand this national character, Europeans initiated projects to write national histories based on the efforts of European and European-trained archaeologists, historians, and other experts. Because most vanquished non-Europeans did not understand themselves in this specific way, it was left to Europeans to "discover" their past and, therefore, make yet another contribution to the progress of the nation. Where previously state power radiated from a ruler's capital and encompassed as many subjects as militarily or politically possible, European ideologies in the service of their empires drew lines that defined the nation and became permanent national borders. In the late eighteenth century, just as the notion of nationalism coalesced in Europe, some North American colonists demonstrated how these currents of thought not only could serve the dominant conquerors but also unify rebellious subjects.

COLONIAL AND NINETEENTH-CENTURY AMERICAN INTERACTIONS WITH MUSLIMS: SLAVERY, DESPOTISM, AND SENSUALITY

At this point in our story, we shift from the general attitudes toward Muslims that arrived with Europeans in America to the specific contacts European Americans had with Muslims in America and abroad. These occurred primarily in the context of either Mediterranean shipping conflicts or the enslavement of African Muslims. However, the prohibition on slave transportation in 1808 and a general intolerance toward non-Christian religions eclipsed whatever little interest whites had in sub-Saharan Muslims. The consistency of the depreciatory depictions of Muslims in cultural expressions of the era reflect the tenaciousness of European views in the new nation even as they suggest the unique perspectives of a changing nation. Overall, three themes dominated this period: Muslims as slaves, as despots, and as sex obsessed or sex objects.

Muslims lived in America before the first English colonists arrived, having already been brought as slaves from Africa by the Spanish.[22] Yet it has taken until recently for scholars to determine that perhaps one of every five Africans enslaved in Africa for transportation to the United States was a Muslim. This demonstrates how completely slavers and the Christianity of slaveholding society erased the religious heritage of slaves. When, in 1976, Alex Haley portrayed his enslaved African ancestor as a Muslim in *Roots*, his fellow historical novelist James Michener criticized him for such an unrealistic characterization.[23] This historical amnesia reflects a general British disinterest, shared by the French, in whether their slaves were Muslim or not and the historical distance these Europeans had traveled since threatened by Muslim armies.

This contrasted with the attitude of the Spanish, who preceded them in introducing African slaves. Spanish colonists in the Americas, informed by a sharper memory of combat with the Iberian Moors, actively sought to exclude Muslim slaves from the New World. They feared that Islamic proselytism might instill resistance among not only slaves but indigenous peoples as well, while undermining Catholic efforts at conversion.[24] Conversion provided a justification central to not only the colonial conquest of indigenous peoples and their resources, but, for some Europeans, their enslavement as well. Meanwhile, Spanish and Portuguese colonists attempted to instill the memory of the Reconquista among their Christianized slaves by requiring them to perform the *Moros y Christianos* play that victoriously reenacted the Christian expulsion of the Muslims from Iberia.[25] In contrast, British Protestants resisted slave conversion until the late eighteenth century because it prompted questions as to whether Christians could be enslaved.[26]

The assumption preferred by British colonists and their descendants was that Africans were inherently unable to be civilized without outside help.[27] If a Muslim African demonstrated abilities in Arabic literacy, then colonists labeled him or her as "Arab," since reading defied African abilities. Whites considered such a quality as evidence of "foreign blood," which made for a respectable difference compared with "true Africans" (not so respectable as to excuse them from enslavement, of course) whom the "Arab" could then be trusted to supervise. This situation reinforced the terrible logic and racial premises of slavery: "Arab Africans" demonstrated capabilities that reflected a bloodline considered white and affirmed white superiority over "true Africans," who, as blacks, deserved slavery.[28] Many English-speaking slaveholders preferred "Mandingo" slaves (those from Senegambia and Sierra Leone) and others from

Muslim-majority regions because of a perceived higher intelligence and European-like facial features that distinguished them from other blacks.[29] A comment by Mark Twain about Abd ar-Rahman reflects that this privileged portrayal of some Muslim Africans did not translate into an overall respect for Muslims. In 1867, Twain viewed the portrait of a Muslim African who had escaped slavery and settled in Liberia. Twain commented on this "dignified old darkey" that "I, for one, sincerely hope that after all his trials he is now peacefully enjoying the evening of his life and eating and relishing the unsaleable niggers from neighboring tribes who fall into his hands."[30] Even if Twain was speaking through his trademark irony, he voiced a disparagement with which he expected his American audience to be familiar, if not hold. However, public recognition of Islam among slaves or former slaves, though never prominent, slowly disappeared; the context of American awareness of Islam and Muslims had already arisen in international relations.

The first international conflict in which the new American republic involved itself took place in the Mediterranean soon after independence. This was a time after the Turkish Ottoman Empire had ended its efforts to expand into Europe yet still controlled a vast area of Mediterranean lands and loomed large in European imaginations. Like many among the British, Americans agreed in their depictions that the Turks lived under a despotic rule that leaned toward anarchy, in large part due to Islam.[31] Turks, and Muslims in general, often served as a negative foil when compared with American ideals. In 1790, John Adams criticized the excesses of the French Revolution by arguing that it would lead the French to "soon wish their books in ashes, seek for darkness and ignorance, superstition and fanaticism, as blessings, and follow the standard of the first mad despot, who, with the enthusiasm of another Mahomet, will endeavor to obtain them." When he thought that Thomas Jefferson included his father's thoughts among "political heresies," John Quincy Adams relied on a common understanding of a militant Muhammad to describe Jefferson as calling on "all true believers in the Islam of democracy to draw their swords." Mocking both the Islamic statement of faith (*shahada*) and Jefferson's excessive support of free thought, Adams depicted him as shouting, "There is one Goddess of Liberty, and Common Sense is her prophet."[32] Regardless of their mutual disagreements, postindependence American politicians could agree that Muslim despotism represented the salient example of what had to be avoided at all costs.³³ They therefore called on this mutually understood negative example to illustrate where the policies of their opponents would lead America, reinforcing the image of inherently despotic Muslims while using the image as an effective rhetorical tool.³⁴

Meanwhile, various states along the North African coast—known to Americans as the Barbary States—demanded tribute of nations whose merchants plied western Mediterranean waters. The states often made captives of men and women aboard the ships of those who defied them, extracting the neglected tribute from the ransom they set. Although many European countries acquiesced, the United States eventually refused, and thus began a series of diplomatic wrangles and naval skirmishes over the next few decades. Relying on the same rhetoric of Muslim despotism and anarchy, American leaders portrayed themselves as uncompromising defenders of liberty in the struggle for free enterprise. They distanced themselves from Europeans who acquiesced to the Barbary extortions and so abetted tyranny. Though Adams and Jefferson may have disagreed on other matters, they could together decry that the "Policy of Christendom has made Cowards of all their Sailors before the Standard of Mahomet."³⁵ The social memory of this early conflict would be instilled in future generations of Americans through the lines of the Marine Corps hymn: "From the halls of Montezuma/To the shores of Tripoli/We will fight our country's battles/In the air, on land, and sea." Meanwhile, Francis Scott Key composed a song celebrating America's ultimate victory. It included the following verses:

> How triumphant they rode, o'er the wandering flood, and stain'd the blue waters with infidel blood
> How mixed with the olive, the laurel did wave, and formed a bright wreath for the brows of the brave.³⁶

A later rewrite that adapted the song to the context of the War of 1812 removed mention of "the Crescent" and "the turban'd head" as symbolic references to the Muslim Tripolitan enemy but retained patriotic mention of "the star-spangled flag." Of course, it was this version that would become the American national anthem. Although the recently independent Americans attempted to distance themselves from their European cousins still caught in the royalist thrall of nondemocratic rule, they continued to reflect European obsession with the Ottomans in which the category "Turk" encompassed all Muslims. In an 1805 instance, New

York newspapers portrayed Tripolitan sailors captured in American naval operations and displayed at various city theaters as "your real *bona fide* imported Turks."[37] Meanwhile, Key's use of the crescent to refer to the Muslim Tripolitans demonstrates the popular American association of what was then a solely Ottoman symbol with Islam universally.

The display of Muslims as visual entertainment represents the third theme in non-Muslim American encounters with Muslims in this period. Undoubtedly the captured "Turks" paraded on stages in New York City drew crowds as tamed representatives of the Ottoman sultan, who, in actuality, exercised little if any influence over the Barbary States. If theirs was the masculine face of the armed might of Muslim despotism, then a feminine face was at least equally an object of fascination since it represented the subjugated victims of Muslim (male) depravity. Fueled by concepts of the Romantic movement that emphasized the "exotic," nineteenth-century European and American depictions of the courts of Muslim rulers rarely missed an opportunity to depict both the tyrant's spear- and sword-armed soldiers and his sensually and scantily clad harem. Artistic schools of realism produced convincing paintings, and later photographs, of women of the harem or seraglio. ("Harem" derives from the Arabic *harim* for "sacred," "forbidden." "Seraglio" derives partly from the Turkish *saray* for "palace.") These satisfied Western appetites for the titillating secrets of forbidden places that teasingly promised prohibited sensual delights. Who could resist? Even the most puritan could nod agreeably at depictions of nude or seminude women enchained to the whims of lascivious men, recognizing the negative morality it demonstrated. The century ended with the World's Fair of 1893 and the arrival of the "hootchy-cootchy" as performed by undulating Algerian dancing women. At a time when stage dancing by women was rare, the "cootch" would become common on stages and carnivals alike.[38] The continued association of "harem" with Arabs and Muslims reflects how skewed knowledge about these people is among English speakers. Not many probably associate the words "algebra," "algorithm," "alcohol," "banana," "coffee," "cotton," "giraffe," and "zenith" with Arabs or Muslims, although they all originated from Arabic.

Advertisers, recognizing an overall American association of sensuality with Muslims, used images of Arabs/Muslims and Arab/Muslim-associated places and objects to market their products. Camel cigarettes, with the eponymous camel standing in front of pyramids, best illustrates this, although other early cigarette brands included Fatima, Mecca,

Medina, and Omar brands. Advertisements often suggested "romance, self-indulgence, or sexual innuendo." In the next century, the new cinema industry would associate these very themes with productions like *The Sheikh* (1921) starring Rudolph Valentino and *The Thief of Baghdad* (1924).[39] Although these movies would have valorous Arab protagonists who represented exotic romance, they also often included villainous, debauched Arabs threatening the female lead. Publicity for the enormously popular *Sheikh* stated, "When an Arab sees a woman he wants to take her" and "See the auction of beautiful girls to the lords of Algerian harems." A condom would later be marketed with the name and an image of an Arab in robes straddling a stallion.[40] The film deliberately connected Arab characters with Islam through depictions of them praying in a mosque. Overall, the effectiveness of the Arab/Muslim in advertising rested in their association with a sensuality bordering on the depraved.

The nineteenth century closed, as it had opened, with American combat against Muslims overseas. The Spanish-American War of 1898, precipitated by Cuban rebellion against their Spanish masters and the sinking of the U.S. battleship *Maine* in Havana harbor, ended with Spanish defeat and the American annexation of the former Spanish possession of the Philippines. President William McKinley explained his decision to a delegation of Methodist clergymen: "There was nothing left for us to do but to take them all, and to educate the Filipinos, and uplift and Christianize them, and by God's grace do the very best we could by them, as our fellow-men for whom Christ also died."[41] Apparently McKinley did not think much of the Christianity of the Filipino Catholic majority. McKinley's successor, Theodore Roosevelt, inherited a rebellion by Filipinos, who were as unwilling to embrace American imperialism as they had been with the Spanish. Roosevelt characterized the opposition in deliberately religious terms as "half-caste Christians, warlike Muslims, and wild pagans,"[42] suggesting that the resistance of the violent Muslim and disorderly pagan was simply in character while local Christians rebelled only due to their half-caste nature. These Muslims continue to be known as *Moros,* the local adaptation of the Spanish *Moor.*

Near the end of the nineteenth century, a more domestic set of encounters began as the first wave of willing Muslim immigrants arrived in the United States. But they, too, would find that their race more than religion determined their status in America. Indeed, these Muslim Syrians and Lebanese arrivals were only a minority among the Christian compatriots with whom they arrived. Their opportunity to naturalize as U.S.

citizens depended on their racial classification and reflected how ambiguous the position of Arabs continued to be for white Americans. Until 1952, federal law followed the Naturalization Act of 1790, which allowed naturalization only to "free white persons and persons of African nativity or descent." Courts made contradictory rulings of Arabs as "yellow," "Caucasian," and "about walnut."[43] Jews faced similarly varied opinions. Although other waves would follow and some Muslims, depending on perceived race, would be accepted as Americans, a popular and unfavorable impression of Muslims as associated with specific ethnicities and inherently different from Americans never seriously diminished. In the middle of the next century, the number of Muslims immigrating to the United States increased tremendously when President Lyndon Johnson ended quotas that restricted most immigration to ethnicities represented already in the country (i.e., Europeans).[44] Paradoxically, these new Americans would arrive just as an increasingly prevalent media image of inexorable conflict between "Islam" and "the West" would more powerfully reflect and reaffirm the generally understood notion that the two were mutually exclusive.

TWENTIETH- AND TWENTY-FIRST-CENTURY INTERACTIONS: SOVIET CONTAINMENT, OIL, ZIONISM, AND TERRORISM

American popular interest in Muslims moved from the incidental interactions and clashes in the nineteenth century to conflicts Americans considered endemic in the twentieth and twenty-first centuries. Economic, religious, and strategic concerns had led American foreign policy and businesses to become very involved in the Middle East at the end of World War II. Few Americans held interest in other Muslim-majority areas. For instance, American tourists did not find South and Southeast Asia until the 1960s. Even then, the cultures and religions that attracted most of these travelers and that supposedly typified these regions were Hindu and Buddhist, not Muslim. This only reaffirmed American impressions of the supposed equivalence of the Middle East and "the Muslim world." Lacking interest in or experience of Muslim-majority cultures to the east of Central Asia where most of the world's Muslims live, Americans continued to imagine all Arabs as Muslim and see all Muslims as Arab, although many Arabs are Christian and only 20 percent of all Muslims are Arab. A vague awareness of the Muslim nature of Middle Easterners became hardened into cold geopolitical fact through American interests in four realms that have become increasingly and unexpectedly interrelated. More elaboration on these interests and the political events that they helped engender can be found in chapter 5.

Soviet Containment

The primary American concern with the world beyond its borders following World War II and until the fall of the Berlin Wall in 1989 was containment of the brawny Soviet Union. The Berlin Wall appeared to be the perfect symbol of the Soviet-NATO divide: a seemingly impenetrable divider that starkly separated two sides into camps demarcated by barbed wire and guard towers. In reality, however, much of the world found itself in a no-man's land stretching between the two sides, enticed by favorable trade agreements and generous military assistance while threatened with arms for opposition parties and penalties in international forums. As early as 1947, President Harry S. Truman declared the nation's willingness to back "free peoples who are resisting subjugation by armed minorities or outside pressures."[45] The world understood that the Truman Doctrine meant more certain support to those facing Soviet pressure than those still wrestling to throw off the remaining vestiges of Western European imperialism.

Neither Americans nor Soviets cared much for the cultural or ideological backgrounds of their proxies, and so, at various times Turkey, Iran, Pakistan, and Egypt became valuable and well-endowed allies of the United States. Their Muslim cultures neither mattered nor were noticed in the popular imagination. All that mattered was whether a country embraced or resisted Soviet Communism, which was characterized as a totalitarianism and an irreligious religion. According to one highly influential government finding, Soviet Communism encouraged individuals to "an act of willing submission . . . under the compulsion of a perverted faith."[46] In order to underscore how America differed, in 1954 the Eisenhower administration inserted the line "one nation, under God" into the Pledge of Allegiance. Meanwhile, the rise of the Pan-Arab movement as resistance to continued British and French regional involvements in the 1950s threatened to unite "the Arab world" without a clear sense whether they would become client states of the West or the Soviets. President Dwight D. Eisenhower understood this and surprised Israel, Britain, and France by not supporting their invasion of Egypt when that country nationalized the Suez Canal. Said he, "How can we possibly support Britain and France if in doing so we were to lose the whole Arab world?"[47] Arab identity, then, was becoming of interest to American audiences. Although understood to be inherently Muslim, this aspect of the Arab identity would not become foremost for Americans until the late 1970s.

Oil

Although during the Cold War Americans sought to entice many nations to enter their sphere of influence, the contest with the Soviets was particularly pointed in the Middle East because of the presence there of the primary fuel of the success of each economy and military: oil. Many of the region's nations already owed their borders and ruling dynasties primarily to European imperial efforts to ensure a politically secure supply of oil once the costs of military occupation became unsustainable. The straight lines of national borders in the Middle East remain as the artifact of these European machinations. The Allies, expecting the Ottoman Empire's demise even before the end of World War I, planned the partition of the Middle East into parcels based almost entirely on their political and economic interests. For instance, at the war's conclusion, the British would meld three oil-rich Ottoman provinces together to establish Iraq.[48] Nearby, they carved out a smaller territory as Kuwait and hand picked the Sabah family as its ruling dynasty. None of these decisions placed any emphasis on the needs, perceptions, or desires of the area's inhabitants. Whereas the less linear borders of Europe reflect how nations there formed through self-determination largely according to local efforts to define a common language and culture, the straight lines of Egypt, Iraq, and other Middle Eastern countries evidence the artifice of European projects to establish nations among peoples who seldom understood themselves according to this European notion of social organization and who, for the most part, did not participate in their own national definition.

American concerns with "Arab oil" heightened only in the 1970s after the Organization of Petroleum Exporting Countries (OPEC) exerted its control over a large percentage of international oil supplies and forced Americans to pay more at the gas pump than they ever imagined. For decades, the United States had built its economy on the assumption of inexpensive oil. Therefore the shocking energy price increases threatened not only the overall economy but also the car culture through which so many Americans expressed their individuality and freedom. Both of these elements made possible such features of the cultural landscape as drive-in diners and movies, Jack Kerouac's *On the Road*, and Ken Kesey's psychedelic magic bus trip that helped define successive generations. OPEC, dominated by Arab states, came to be seen not simply as an economic competitor in the capitalist marketplace but a cultural opponent to America that threatened "the American lifestyle." The immediate occasion for the 1973 oil embargo that first signaled the rise of this threat was American support for Israel in the 1973 October War.

Zionism

It seems odd to imagine that Jewish nationalists once considered Madagascar as a serious candidate for a Jewish state. In the years preceding World War I, many sites, including Palestine, were considered. Even after the League of Nations included provisions for the establishment of a Jewish national home when they established the British Mandate in Palestine in 1922, some Jews rejected the concept out of hand as either unnecessary due to European Christian tolerance or, especially among the Orthodox, impious in light of the Messiah's expected reestablishment of the kingdom of David. However, the unparalleled horrors of the Holocaust silenced all meaningful opposition in the West, including that of other Jews, and the settlers who lived under the auspices of the British Mandate prepared to declare an independent Israel once the war-weary British departed in 1948. Many local and regional Arabs resisted the establishment of Israel. This culminated in four outright wars in 1948, 1956, 1967, and 1973 between Israel and some Arab states and a persistent tension between Israeli Jews (Israeli Arabs are few) and Palestinians (which includes Christians among a majority Muslim population) that continues to generate violence and victims.

American support for Israel, unmatched in tenacity by any other nation, resulted from a variety of factors. First, many American Jews considered the Holocaust as justification enough for a Jewish state: the final evidence that Jews needed a self-established nation as a sanctuary in a world in which no nation dominated by Gentiles could be entirely trusted and no people fully recognized unless organized into a nation-state. A great many also felt an overwhelming guilt at their perceived inaction during—or even their survival of—the Shoah and found an outlet for their feelings through support for Israel via Washington lobbyists. Second, Israel offered to be a bulwark in the anti-Communist system of alliances in a region critical to American economic interests. Third, Israel represented a nation far more familiar in outline, at least in its initial decades, to Americans than its regional neighbors: founded on biblical and frontier myths, democratic ideals, and European sensibilities. Anti-Jewish sentiment in the United States, which had become particularly pronounced in the 1930s as Americans sought scapegoats for the Great Depression, was neutralized in American support for a Jewish land heroically wrested from Arab hands.

Although the American media today commonly depicts the Israeli-Palestinian conflict as one between Jews and Muslims, this is not the way those involved have always understood it. The regional support for Palestinians would originally—and, in large part, still does—gravitate around a shared Arab identity. The European origin of most of the first Zionist settlers prompted Arabs to consider this as a final act of colonization in the two-hundred-year drama of European imperial control. In the eyes of many Arabs, these Jewish settlers represented the last remnant of European Jewish populations that Christians had failed to annihilate and now wanted relocated from their countries. For Arabs, this quality of the conflict became more Islamic in orientation with the Israeli capture of the Temple Mount/al-Aqsa Mosque in 1967 and the demise of the Palestinian Liberation Organization (P.L.O.) and its perennial leader, Yasser Arafat, as a credible vehicle of resistance. Hamas and other organizations that defined themselves through Islamic ideologies ascended. American bonds with Israel appeared to be palpably tightened with the September 11 attacks, sharing in the persistent threat of Islamic terrorism.

TERRORISM

It will be nearly impossible for the American reader to consider the matter of Muslims and terrorism without the attacks of September 11, 2001, as the starting point for any discussion. The monumental shock of this catastrophic event—as absolute in its unexpectedness as it was complete in its devastation—has led many observers to agree that the world irrevocably changed as a result. Although others around the world, especially those who have long suffered the imminent threat of violence from opposition groups, may be impatient with what they consider an American naïveté regarding terrorism, the impact of the event remains seminal. The deeply felt American vulnerability to an Islamic threat, the use of this in the justification for U.S. aggression abroad, and the soaring suspicion of the United States among Muslims globally are all on a higher level of magnitude from previous events. Nothing before had so crystallized fears of Muslims and Islam: not the 444-day confinement of American embassy staff by Iranian students (1979), the deaths of hundreds of U.S. Marines in Lebanon due to Hezbollah suicide car bombers (1983), the Ayatollah Khomeini's *fatwa* (legal ruling) consigning author Salman Rushdie to death for his novel *The Satanic Verses* (1989), nor the first bombing of the World Trade Center (1993).

As terrorism has become one of the defining issues of both domestic and foreign policy in the United States in the twenty-first century, Muslims have become nearly synonymous with the term in the minds of many Americans. This represents a significant change from earlier decades, when groups that attacked civilians tended to be viewed as nationalist movements. For instance, throughout much of the last half of the twentieth century, the American media portrayed Arab organizations as among a variety of terrorist movements that included those run by Nicaraguans, West Germans, Puerto Ricans, Filipinos, Italians, and Irishmen and women. Palestinian groups, for instance, embarked upon a series of crimes, often murderous, to gain global attention to their causes. The Palestinian Liberation Organization hijacked airliners, and, perhaps most infamously, Black September slew Israeli athletes during the 1972 Munich Olympics. However, despite the predominantly Muslim composition of the P.L.O., it was more likely to be identified by Americans as Arab than Muslim at least until the 1980s. American news outlets have portrayed the subsequent rise of Hamas as the result of an Islamic surge among Palestinians, shifting the focus from nationalist struggle to religious fanaticism despite the Palestinians' undiminished desire for a self-determined state.

After the tragic disasters of September 11, non-Muslim American responses toward Muslims in the United States have varied. Many Muslims, their homes, businesses, and mosques suffered threats and, sometimes, even assault by outraged fellow citizens. However, other non-Muslim Americans have redoubled their efforts at interfaith communication as Muslims increase their attempts to educate the general population about Islam while condemning the crimes. Islamic organizations ran out of outreach materials in the next year as they scrambled to answer questions about Islam and Muslim lives. The presence of these domestic groups reflects both the rising numbers of American Muslims and their increasing organizing efforts to counter anti-Islamic and anti-Muslim perceptions. Unfortunately, although some non-Muslims have attempted to emphasize the spirit of "charity which we owe to each other," as Pope Gregory VII described at the turn of the last millennium, the overall impression that dominated earlier of Muslims and Islam as a barbarous, expanding, oppressive force has found apparent reinforcement in the minds of many—perhaps most—Americans since the events of 2001.

• 2 •

Symbols of Islam, Symbols of Difference

$\mathcal{S}$imply put, symbols are objects and images that represent something else. So, for instance, VW in a circle symbolizes Volkswagen, H_2O symbolizes water, and the cross symbolizes Christianity. National symbols are perhaps more ubiquitous than most: the maple leaf symbolizes Canada; the rising sun, Japan; the Star of David, Israel; and the bear, Russia. Americans refer to the United States using a number of symbols: the bald eagle, the Stars and Stripes, and Uncle Sam. In addition, the Capitol Building and White House represent the government, the Constitution its political ideals, the Statue of Liberty its self-conception as a beacon of freedom.

Every symbol relies on the agreement among a group of people that when they see the object or image, it will represent something else to them. Some symbols, like those mentioned above, result from a group determining that a symbol will stand for the group. But some symbols are created by one party to refer to another, which may or may not embrace the symbol used. So, for instance, Nazi Germans required gays and lesbians to wear the inverted pink triangle on their clothing, having invented this as a symbol of their victims' queerness.[1]

Political cartoons rely on symbols as a shorthand by which the reader can understand to whom the cartoonist refers. The artist must clearly establish whom she is commenting upon in the very limited space afforded most cartoons. Symbols effectively conserve space because without the use of any words or excessive images, a people, an object, an idea, a corporation, or a religion can be immediately signified as being part of the issue. The symbols connoting Islam and Muslims chosen by American political cartoonists primarily derive from American and

45

European experiences of Middle Eastern Muslims, therefore projecting onto all Muslims symbols that, by and large, do not derive from their own self-understanding.

This chapter examines these symbols so we can understand how they work and what they communicate about American perceptions of Muslims and Islam. Their full importance becomes clearer in the more detailed analysis we will undertake in later chapters. The use of "Islamic" symbols by contemporary cartoonists demonstrates that even when Americans did not consciously associate Middle Eastern political activity with Islam, they have often equated all Muslims with the Middle East and all Muslims with Islam. This chapter contrasts these depictions with a consideration of American political cartoonists' use of symbols depicting their own country.

It is important to keep in mind the distinction between symbols of Islam and caricatures of Muslims. The next chapter will consider how cartoonists have caricatured Muslims—drawn Muslims in ways the cartoonist assumes his or her reader will recognize. Caricatures are not symbols because they operate under the assumption that the representation physically resembles, even if in an embellished manner, the person or people to whom it refers. No one assumes that all Americans look like Uncle Sam or Ms. Liberty. One does expect that a caricature of the serving president will resemble in a perhaps exaggerated way the president's actual appearance. This difference will become more important in the next chapter when we examine the widespread use of caricature in American cartoons to represent Muslims in a way that finds little parallel with caricatures of Americans—or, for that matter, Christians and Jews.

THE SCIMITAR

Although the Arab defenders in the Levant used straight-edged swords for the first two centuries of the Crusades, as was the norm among Crusaders, Western cultural memory forgets this.[2] Instead, the sharply curved scimitar[3] became a primary symbol of difference, marking the supposed chasm between the Arab Muslims and the European Christians as seen in any number of Hollywood films. This may have become the case, in part, because one European weapon—the cruciform-shaped long sword—served many Crusaders as symbolic of their movement since it was so similar to the central emblem of Christianity: the cross.

The irony of the negative symbolism of the scimitar is that different branches of the U.S. armed forces have armed themselves with curved-bladed swords in imitation of these weapons. George S. Patton, while still in the horse cavalry and long before he became one of the last century's most famous generals, noted that the contemporary American cavalry saber directly descended from the Arab "curved scimitar-like saber."[4] U.S. Marine Corps officers continue to wear the ceremonial Mameluke scimitar sword in symbolic memory of the 1805 campaign on the "shores of Tripoli" when a desert chieftain gifted one to the Marines' commanding officer.[5] Meanwhile, the Air Force named two jet fighters "Sabre," and the word even was taken as the name of Buffalo's ice hockey team. Nevertheless, American cartoonists reserve the scimitar as a symbol of Muslim barbarity, repeatedly showing it in the hands or by the sides of unjustifiably violent characters, yet seldom, if ever, in their depictions of the American military.

Jack Ohman, 2004. ©2004 Tribune Media Services, Inc.

In this cartoon, Jack Ohman weaves together the phenomenon of beheadings—currently associated in the minds of many Americans with the violence and lawlessness of Islamic fundamentalism—with the implied threat of the scimitar. Although cartoonists occasionally put outsized scimitars in Muslim hands to make them appear comically barbaric, this specific example pictures a scimitar communicating a serious threat. Its presence serves to inform the reader that the response to revelations of American abuse of Iraqi captives in the Abu Ghraib prison will be distinctly foreign, perhaps Arab, and certainly violent.

THE MOSQUE

Muhammad directed the building of the first historical mosque soon after Muslims settled in Medina and established the first Islamic society. Since then, the mosque has served most Muslim cultures as a place for communal prayer. The call to prayer often emanates from the top of a minaret that commonly, though not always, stands attached to the mosque. Reflecting the egalitarian impulses of Islam, most mosques encompass a courtyard open to the sky and a fully enclosed space that allows the devout to stand side by side during their prayers no matter what the weather brings. However, this egalitarianism applies almost exclusively to men in many Muslim cultures, and women remain excluded from a great many mosques due to patriarchal concerns for the purity of the mosque (possibly compromised by a menstruating woman) and the concentration of men (possibly troubled by the presence of prostrating women).

Understandably, American cartoonists have seized upon the mosque as a symbol of a people's Islamic character since it serves as the most conspicuous place of Islamic prayer (although many Muslims also pray in their homes and businesses). Of course, mosques stand on almost every continent, but they figure into cartoon skylines as an indicator of the otherness of a place if the cartoonist wants to indicate that the setting is a place inhabited predominantly by Muslims. The onion-domed shadow of the stereotyped mosque commonly looms in the background of cartoons of Iranian, Iraqi, or Egyptian cities, marking the space and its people as Muslim. Although many cities in these countries do indeed have mosques, their inclusion in American cartoons serves less to provide some realistic portrayal of a cityscape (that would not serve the car-

WE'VE LOOKED EVERYWHERE FOR BIN LADEN, AND ALL WE CAN FIND ARE OPPRESSED WOMEN, JAILED CHRISTIANS, HUNGRY CHILDREN, EXECUTED ADULTERERS, TERRIFIED DISSENTERS AND MEN OF GOD.

toonist's editorial goals) than to symbolize the presumed Muslim and/or Arab character of the people.

The prominence in cartoons of the mosque as a symbol for both the Middle East and Islam cannot be overstated. This demonstrates an American perception that Middle Easterners are almost always Muslim. As Muslims, they are expected to adhere to a set of beliefs that, the cartoonist suggests, causes them to behave differently from his mainstream American audience.

In this cartoon, the minaret stands in for the whole mosque while doubling as a watchtower for armed Taliban. It symbolizes the violence of, if not all Islam, the Taliban's interpretation of it as reflected in their "discoveries."

THE CRESCENT

Few Europeans or Americans have heard the tale that the croissant they eat for breakfast originated among Viennese bakers in 1689 in celebration of the Turkish failure that year to seize the city after a long siege. The act of eating croissants (French for "crescent") was a symbolic act perpetrated, according to folklore, against the crescent symbol of the vanquished Ottomans, who also abandoned their supply of coffee, which supposedly became the foundation of that famous Viennese brew.[6] At that time, however, few of the world's Muslims would have associated their religion with this symbol. How the crescent (often with a star perched between its two horns) came to be considered three hundred years later as a universal symbol of Islam remains historically unclear.

What is known is that in the nineteenth century the Ottomans—the last of the great Muslim-run empires—adopted the crescent moon in their effort to fashion a nationalist flag comparable to those of its European neighbors. Today, at least eleven Muslim-majority countries—as far from the old Ottoman lands as Malaysia—include a crescent moon on their national flags. Meanwhile, the Red Cross established the Red Crescent in answer to Muslim concerns of insensitivity and exclusion on behalf of the international organization. Despite these adoptions by

Problems in Revenge

...for example, to retaliate for an attack on two of the tallest buildings in America, we could attack two of the tallest buildings in Afghanistan...

Jeff Danziger, 2001. Jeff Danziger, New York Times Syndicate

IT BECAME NECESSARY TO DESTROY THE CITY TO SAVE IT.

Paul Conrad, 2004. ©2004 Tribune Media Services, Inc.c.

some Muslims, others reject the crescent as a symbol of Islam because they reject the use of all religious symbols.

Many political cartoonists use the crescent moon, like the mosque, to act as a symbol associating places and people with Islam and/or Muslims. The otherness of Afghanistan as depicted by cartoonist Jeff Danziger is marked not only by the diminutive "tallest buildings" barely rising above the rubble of the city but also by the distant crescent moon atop the dome of what is presumably a mosque.

A comparison of the deliberately designated Muslim space in Danziger's cartoon with the undifferentiated any-city portrait of Paul Conrad's image raises two important questions. Does Conrad omit all symbolic differences that would differentiate an Iraqi city from an American one in order to better promote both empathy for the destroyed city and his criticism of American attacks?[7] Conversely, does Danziger include the mosque as a mark of difference so as to emotionally distance his audience from the targets—architectural and human—of American bombing?

MUSLIM MEN

Ironically, unless cartoonists intend to depict the oppressiveness of Islam toward women, they will most likely use the figure of a man or collection of men as a symbol of Islam. In an odd reenactment of the very patriarchal focus on men that they so often criticize in Islam, most American cartoonists exclude women as symbols of the religion.

This would surprise and alarm many Muslim women (and men), who understand that women play a critical role maintaining Muslim cultures and continuing Islamic practices and beliefs. Even in the most patriarchal of Muslim societies (patriarchy, of course, not being limited to Muslim cultures), women consider Islam to be fully their concern and duty too, not just the purview of the local mullah or imam or of the men in their family. Some of these men have more authority than any women to interpret religious dictates, but women still actively fashion their own practice and teach children what their mothers taught them.[8]

Glenn McCoy, 2001. GLENN MCCOY 2001 Belleville News-Democrat. Reprinted with permission of UNIVERSAL PRESS SYNDICATE. All rights reserved.

In the image above, cartoonist Glenn McCoy depicts four nearly identical men as "Islam." They wear physically indistinguishable turbans, black shirts, and pants. Of course, the gigantic and fire-bound head of bin Laden merely mirrors the faces we see in profile, at best. All but one of the four has a beard and holds a book or scroll. The usage of only homogeneous men to represent Islam suggests various generalizations to the reader. On a basic level, we have the physical: although many pious Muslim men do wear headgear out of respect for Allah and grow beards in imitation of the Prophet Muhammad, such is not universally the case. Also clear is the intimation that religious Islam is defined by men. But perhaps more insidious is the notion that terrorist organizations like bin Laden's can dupe and befoul the entire religion. The presence of Satan connects more subtly with Christian accusations that demonic forces manipulated Muslims, as we shall see in chapter 5.

THE VEIL

If a generalized image of a Muslim man comes to represent all of Islam—and subsequently all the negative stereotypes that accrue to the

Paul Conrad, 2004. ©2004 Tribune Media Services, Inc.

religion—a much more specific marker is used to symbolize Muslim oppression with regard to women. As mentioned earlier, cartoonists almost never symbolize Islam or Muslims with images of women. When females do appear, they are almost always depicted as veiled and oppressed. The veil, then, and not a woman, symbolizes Islam and its implied oppressiveness. In other words, it is the invisibility of a woman, seldom her presence, that symbolizes Islam. Islam, through this symbol, can only be considered as inherently lacking.

Paul Conrad's arresting cartoon superimposes two symbols in one intentionally frightening image. It serves simultaneously as a caution against both the oppression of women and the threat of Muslims with nuclear technology.

The twin obsessions of oppressed Muslim women and violent Muslim men find clear expression in the cartoon below. Using the assumed normality of Barbie and Ken, Walt Handelsman depicts the Saudi-approved Burqa Barbie and Jihad Ken with mocking derision of the society that these figures symbolize.

Overall, then, symbols of Islam used by American cartoonists set Muslims and their settings apart from what the cartoonists presume American audiences consider normal. In their efforts to symbolize Islam and Muslims for the ease of reader identification, they both demonstrate and reinforce the broad generalizations about Muslims with which their audiences are already familiar.

Although no reader would assume that Islam is as compact or tangible as a single mosque, Ben Sargent's cartoon nevertheless implies that one man, in this case Osama bin Laden, can hijack a religion associated with at least 1.2 billion people throughout the world. Even allowing for the constraints of space and necessary brevity of comment, the cartoon's contention defies tenable argument. Yet the presumed difference of and lack of experience with Islam undoubtedly makes it possible for many

Walt Handelsman, 2003. © 2003 Tribune Media Services, Inc.

Ben Sargent, 2001. SARGENT © 2001 Austin American-Statesman. Reprinted with permission of UNIVERSAL PRESS SYNDICATE. All rights reserved.

Americans to accept the portrayed singularity of the religion and the uniformity of those who adhere to it. Even the most critical American would be unlikely to take seriously a similar image of "Christianity" in the thrall of a single conservative Christian like Jerry Falwell.

The ultimate result of such universalizations, hinted at in the following Chuck Asay cartoon, is nondifferentiation and broad bias. One interpretation of this cartoon suggests that Asay conflates the al Qaeda group in Saudi Arabia that brutally murdered American contractor Paul Johnson with all those incarcerated by American forces in Iraqi and Afghan prisons and Guantánamo Bay—despite their diversity in nation of origin and degree of innocence. If this reading is correct, then the cartoon considers the allegations of prisoner abuse to pale alongside the murder because all of the prisoners are "these animals." If so, this demonstrates how the universalizing of symbols can slide so easily into caricature and stereotype, as described in the next chapter, while justifying normally unjustifiable behavior such as sleep deprivation.

Another outcome of overgeneralization is the straightforward equation of all Muslims with violence. In many cartoons, a caricature of "the

Chuck Asay, 2004. By permission of Chuck Asay and Creators Syndicate, Inc

Muslim" becomes the symbol of terrorism itself. In Ben Sargent's cartoon below, "Terrorism" labels a bearded man who wears both a vest and hat common to Pathan men in Afghanistan and Pakistan. Sargent does not label the second figure, expecting that almost any reader will identify the character as Uncle Sam, who has served as a symbol of the United States for more than a century. The cartoon, therefore, usefully demonstrates that the image of "a Muslim" does not necessarily symbolize terrorism. If it did, there would be no need to label the figure, just as there is no need to label Uncle Sam. However, Sargent connects Muslims to the character representing terrorism by dressing him in a way that his audience will associate with Muslims. After all, he could have drawn the figure as wearing a dress shirt and pants, which terrorists—Muslim or not—would be more likely to wear than the traditional clothing of Pathan men. Instead, Sargent explicitly denotes the supposedly Muslim quality of terrorism.

It is important to note that while the person used to depict "terrorism" in this example symbolizes Muslims because of his resemblance to the American image of a Muslim man, Uncle Sam symbolizes the

United States not because of his physical resemblance to Americans but because of American familiarity with this symbol, who is partially identified by his clothes decorated with the stars and stripes of the U.S. flag. This use of symbols for the United States by American cartoonists bears further examination in order to better demonstrate how this differs from the symbolization of Muslims and Islam.

UNCLE SAM AND LADY LIBERTY

The frequency with which readers see these depictions of Muslims inures many to their insidious nature. Moreover, the implicitly humorous character of political cartoons—which spend more time satirizing non-Muslims than Muslims—may seem to make criticism of their depreciatory depiction of Muslims too thin-skinned, especially in light of the skeptical tone implicit in most cartoons. However, a closer look at American cartoonists' use of Uncle Sam and the Statue of Liberty as

Ben Sargent, 2001. SARGENT © 2001 Austin American-Statesman. Reprinted with permission of UNIVERSAL PRESS SYNDICATE. All rights reserved.

symbols for the United States demonstrates important insights regarding their treatment of Americans relative to Muslims. Each of these symbols has long personified the American people and their highest ideals, although in divergent ways.

Americans have, for more than a century, considered Uncle Sam as one of the most symbolic figures for their country. It is not by coincidence that he shares the same initials as the United States. Cartoonists overwhelmingly picture him as the older, straight-shouldered, white-bearded man as he was portrayed in the famous recruiting poster for World War I, in which he pointed at the viewer and exclaimed, "I want *you* for the U.S. Army" (see figure on p. 57). However, cartoonists do not limit their depictions of Uncle Sam to the big and brawny. He may be diminutive in size, quizzical in appearance, or downright naive, depending on the context in which the artist situates him.

Tom Toles, 2003. TOLES © 2003 The Washington Post. Reprinted with permission of UNIVERSAL PRESS SYNDICATE. All rights reserved.

For example, Tom Toles's slight and innocent Uncle Sam contrasts with the burly and determined Uncle Sam that graced many cartoons immediately following 9/11. The contrast between such depictions shows how cartoonists intend to express some character of Americans in general through what Uncle Sam does or says or how Uncle Sam appears. If Uncle Sam moves forcefully, it is because the United States moves forcefully. If Uncle Sam appears confounded, it is because the nation is so. But nowhere do artists intentionally portray Uncle Sam as some realistic depiction of what Americans look like, beyond his near universal rendering as white.

The same is true with the Statue of Liberty, which has also served as a symbol of America and its values since the late nineteenth century. However, Ms. Liberty usually communicates different dimensions of the American character than Uncle Sam. The difference is a gendered one. Whereas Uncle Sam usually connotes strength, Lady Liberty obviously symbolizes the ideal of liberty. Therefore, in situations where this ideal is seemingly under attack, it makes sense that we often see her as the beleaguered target. But more importantly, it is Liberty's feminine aspect

NOW THINK... WHAT COULD YOU HAVE DONE TO PROVOKE THIS ATTACK?

Glenn McCoy, 2002. GLENN MCCOY 2002 Belleville News-Democrat. Reprinted with permission of UNIVERSAL PRESS SYNDICATE. All rights reserved.

that comes to represent the victimized, delicate counterpart to Uncle Sam's heroic, strong male protector.

In relying upon this dichotomy, cartoonists often reflect the patriarchal sentiments of mainstream American culture that still, after a century of feminist agitation and consciousness-raising, commonly casts men as protective leaders and women as vulnerable victims. The parallel is not serendipitous. Once again we are reminded that representations of others often say far more about the unconscious cultural assumptions of the cartoonists than the cultural realities of those they satirize.

• 3 •

Stereotyping Muslims and Establishing the American Norm

*E*ven before *The Siege* was released in 1998, the film's producers faced protests regarding its depiction of Muslims and Islam. They responded by arguing that the film actually shows Muslims in a good light, not a negative one. The difference between these two perspectives is illustrative of the dynamics of stereotyping and the power of "the norm."

The film, with eerie foreshadowing, focuses on the efforts of the Federal Bureau of Investigation to combat Islamic terrorists who are killing civilians for the sake of media coverage. Tony Shalhoub costars as a Muslim Arab American serving as an agent; his superior is played by Denzel Washington. The director obviously intended to provoke the audience's sympathy for Shahloub's character, especially at the point in the plot when the city comes under martial law enforced by a ruthless general, played by Bruce Willis, who creates internment camps for the city's Muslim men, including the son of Shalhoub's character. So what's objectionable about the film? Careful consideration of the visual depiction of the two primary Muslim characters—the FBI agent and the chief terrorist—reveals themes that, however unintentional on the part of the producers, demonstrate some of the dynamics of Islamophobia.

At first glance, the film appears to promote a positive image of Muslims. The most prominent difference between the Muslim terrorist and the Muslim agent is obvious: The first kills hapless civilians while the second protects them. This parallels the difference between the army general and the FBI superior; the former imprisons innocent Muslim New Yorkers, while the latter protects them. The film clearly, and understandably, defines terrorist violence and martial law as antagonistic to normal American life. Enemies to this norm, the film declares, can be found among Americans as well as among foreigners, and among Muslims as well as among non-Muslims. Muslims, including the courageous Arab American agent, can be part of this norm that ideally refects the multireligious and multiethnic reality of America, as evidenced by the African American FBI chief and various European American characters.

However, another difference exists between the two Muslim characters, one that undermines this message of Muslim inclusion in the American norm. This difference derives from the role of Islam in each character's life: The favorably depicted FBI agent never does anything that would associate him with Islam, while the terrorist frequently performs acts deriving from the religion. The only images of *salat* (the formal Islamic prayer involving standing, bowing, kneeling, and prostration) occur when the terrorist prepares to kill. The only references to Islamic beliefs occur in situations of violent conflict. The agent identifies himself as a Muslim only in the context of defining himself as not like the terrorists; otherwise he says and does nothing associated with Islam. In other words, he acts "normally": that is, like the other Americans in the film, who also make no reference—verbal or physical—to their religion, if indeed they have any. The terrorists, with their solemn prayers and angry declarations, all act aberrantly to this secular norm. Significantly, too, the general played by Willis warns against entrusting the military with control of the city because he recognizes the abuse of power that might, and does, result. However, the Islamic terrorist demonstrates a total absence of regret, remorse, or restraint. Ultimately, religious beliefs and acts not only distinguish the terrorists, they motivate the terrorists' irrational violence. The implicit message, then, is that Muslims who do not act religiously can be good, normal Americans, while Muslims who perform Islamic rituals and espouse Islamic beliefs also commit terrorist acts.

It should not come as a surprise that a character acting on religious impulse would be depicted negatively in a mainstream American film. Relatively few movies include characters who participate in organized religion. For those that do—and do so in non-Christian communities— religion often motivates dark behavior (e.g., *Indiana Jones and the Temple of Doom, The Mummy*). The exception would be Hollywood portrayals of practicing Buddhists, which are almost uniformly favorable (e.g., *Lost Horizon, Seven Years in Tibet, Kundun*). All the more significant, then, that *The Siege* includes only two religiously self-identified characters and that the hero distinguishes himself as on the side of angels by acting nonreligiously while publicly subordinating his Muslim identity to his American identity. The very presence of the Muslim hero—and the producers' promotion of the positiveness of his role—reflect the studio's expectation that American audiences implicitly equate Muslims with violence and therefore need a counterexample to show otherwise. Ambiguous portrayals of Christian faith in modern films (e.g., *The Godfather* trilogy, *The Apostle*, *21 Grams*) also have flawed Christian protagonists—but express no such need for balance.

The lesson of *The Siege* is that when one describes others as being aberrant, one relies on an audience's implicit understanding of what is normal. The Other is distinguished from "us" by characteristics that "they" have (and, implicitly, "we" do not; e.g., disunity, wickedness, irrationality). Or they may be distinguishable by characteristics "they" lack (e.g., civilization, restraint, morality) that "we" presumably have. So the qualities that the person making the distinction uses usually reflect what is considered normal or natural to the group with which he or she associates—or, more specifically, with him- or herself. If you were to describe someone to a friend, you'd be unlikely to characterize that person as someone with two eyes—unless, perhaps, neither you nor your friend had two eyes—because this characterization would not seem distinctive enough to help the other person very much. On the other hand, if the person being described had only one eye, you might be tempted to describe her by this distinctive feature. In the end, the ways in which one describes others often implicitly describe oneself at the same time. This becomes particularly obvious with stereotypes.

Stereotypes are simply descriptions of a group by outsiders using characteristics understood both to be shared by all members and to define them as different from "normal" society. These characteristics may be physical (e.g., tall), behavioral (e.g., excitable), or moral (e.g., conservative). Stereotypes often generate specific symbols of difference from the norm. Undoubtedly, the complaint many Muslims had about *The Siege* arose from its assumption that performing Islamic rituals should be a distinction that costs one membership in the norm by immediately triggering the suspicion connected to a negative stereotype. In other words, many Muslims felt that the film made the Islamic ritual washing and prayer symbolic of terrorism and feared that these symbols of Islam would register as antithetical to the American norm.

How could the presumably non-Muslim producers of the film not understand this? Norms work by establishing expectations so fundamental to a society that they operate invisibly; or at least, they remain invisible to most of those who fit the parameters of normality. An exercise in imaginative inversion helps these norms become visible to those who take them for granted. So, for instance, how would most American men see their position in society if only women had ever been elected as president and vice president of the United States? In another inversion, we might wonder how European Americans would see the legal system if all but two Supreme Court justices had been African American. How would it seem to most Americans if Passover, not Christmas, was a national holiday?

These exercises are not intended to deny that Christian European Americans make up the largest demographic group in the country but rather, by putting the shoe on the other foot, to make apparent the inequalities stemming from majority rule that many, if not most, Americans take for granted. This helps those who fit the norm recognize how the nation seems to many of those who do not. Tragically, many of those excluded from the privileges associated with being "normal" accept the norm that undermines their self-esteem and sense of worth. Often they try to downplay or, if possible, erase the differences that distinguish them. Some immigrants anglicize their names, some southerners "lose their accents," and some gays "act straight." In part in recognition of and resistance to this dynamic, Malcolm X chose a separatist strategy in addressing racial inequality in the United States, rejecting the integrationist efforts of the civil rights movement, and criticizing Dr. Martin Luther King Jr. because Malcolm X did not believe that whites, no matter what other concessions they might offer, would ever give up their power to define the norm. It is perhaps not incidental that he embraced the Nation of Islam, and later Sunni Islam, as part of his effort to convince blacks of their worth outside of white norms.

It is similarly important to establish that the norm is not necessarily a reflection of the majority. Women outnumber men in the United States and yet moviegoers expect more male heroes than female. Meanwhile, whites will soon be a minority in the country, yet white performers are the norm in television, film, and video depictions of American life. Norms reflect the privilege of being taken as the standard of the everyday, and those who establish this standard of normality are able to do so because they have more power than other groups. Again, many may exercise that power and privilege without ever recognizing it as such because norms often operate invisibly to those fortunate enough to find themselves comfortably within their bounds. Some may decide to revolt against the strictures norms require (e.g., speaking "articulately," behaving "properly," dressing "appropriately"), but theirs is the luxury to reject what others may never be privy to no matter what they do or say.

And so, in the consideration of stereotyping that follows, it is worthwhile to consider how cartoonists have depicted people as Muslim through caricatures meant to immediately signal to the audience, through specific symbols, that Muslims stand outside of the accepted norm. Many social groups have struggled with stereotyping in the mass media that has straitjacketed them in specific roles within the norm. For decades, directors cast African Americans only when they wanted to portray the impoverished, the criminal, or the enslaved. Mexican Americans found work performing primarily as banditos, Mexican soldiers, and illegal immigrants. And, of course, women have long struggled to play more varied roles in film than mothers, sisters, wives, lovers, prostitutes, and short-lived victims. According to the movies, the typical police officer, soldier, lawyer, doctor, investigative reporter, or FBI agent has been for a very long time a European American male of uncertain (meaning not conspicuous) religion.

FROM CARICATURE TO STEREOTYPE

Caricature is the practice by which artists focus on one or more unusual physical or behavioral features of an individual, and exaggerate those characteristics in their portrayal.[1] The desired effect of caricature is to satirize the individual. The audience must recognize both the individual being ridiculed and the meaning the cartoonist is communicating regarding the individual's actions or character. This is generally done through popularly recognizable symbols. For instance, the noses of dishonest politicians are prolonged in a Pinocchio-like fashion, adulterers are given horns, and those perceived as cunning have their eyes slanted and faces elongated in a fox-like manner.[2] Or a cartoonist may settle into a standard caricature of a person, exaggerating what may already be unusual characteristics in order to quicken the reader's identification of the individual, as with Richard Nixon's hanging jowls, Jimmy Carter's large smile, and Ronald Reagan's pompadour.

In the artist's challenge to portray a political situation and his or her opinions about it in a very small space with far fewer words than are available to the editorial columnist, caricature is a necessary strategy. However, when this caricature of an individual according to unique physical and behavioral characteristics relies on the assumed characteristics of an entire people, the caricature slides into the realm of stereotype.

The term "stereotype" originated in the publishing industry, referring to the print block from which identical prints were repeatedly produced without variation.[3] Walter Lippmann, in his seminal treatise on the media, *Public Opinion*, changed the meaning of the term into its current usage. He explained how stereotypes work: "We notice a trait which marks a well known type, and fill in the rest of the picture by means of the stereotypes we carry about in our heads." He noted, however, "the pictures inside people's heads do not automatically correspond with the world outside." In other words, what people associate—positively or

Ann Telnaes, 2004. © 2004 Ann Telnaes. Reprint permission granted by Ann Telnaes and Creators Syndicate. All rights reserved.

negatively—with the stereotyped group often comes from their own society rather than an experience with that group.[4]

Like a symbol, as described in the previous chapter, the stereotype works because when viewers encounter one, they associate a great deal more with it than the simple depiction itself offers. The above cartoon amply demonstrates the differences between symbol, caricature, and stereotype. In it, cartoonist Ann Telnaes uses a camel, oil derricks, and onion-domed minarets to symbolize Saudi Arabia and prompt reader associations of desert life, oil wealth, and Islam with the kingdom. Telnaes uses caricatures of former president George H. W. Bush (exaggerating his characteristically large chin and glasses), President George W. Bush (with large ears and prominent eyebrows), Vice President Dick Cheney (with a dour expression on his small mouth), and Secretary of State Condoleezza Rice (unhappy and hard faced). Telnaes expects readers to identify them through these characteristics, and so does not label the individuals with their names. The depiction of the Saudi man differs because he represents something quite apart from the specific individuals found in the portrayal of the Americans.

Instead of depicting the Saudi king or government ministers who could be labeled with their names or positions for reader identification, the cartoonist opts instead for a single stereotyped Saudi. He sits with the politicians—corpulent, bearded, and mustachioed, and wearing the Arab dress of kaffiyeh headdress and *thobe* (the long robe-like clothing worn by many Arab men). Whereas the Americans wear the kaffiyeh and sit "Indian style" to symbolize their collaboration with the Saudis, the Saudi man dons these as part of the stereotype of all Saudi men.

No doubt, few enjoy the caricatures cartoonists make of them. Anyone who has spent time on a grade-school playground knows how it feels to have someone draw attention and exaggerate one's distinctive physical or behavioral qualities. Such are the hazards of a public life. However, caricatures or stereotypes of whole groups risk causing greater injury than dented egos. Instead of an individual made readily identifiable through specific characteristics, stereotypes lead to universalizations that label all individuals who deliberately or accidentally manifest some or all of the stereotyped characteristics. This forces an identification on these persons, none of whom may understand themselves in this manner.

A stereotype of Muslim men relies on the characteristics of the beard and mustache, kaffiyeh or turban, and brown skin. In the week

AP images. Permission also granted by the individual under arraignment.

immediately following the September 11 tragedy, scores of incidents in-volving police arrests and public harassment of not only Muslims but also Sikh men occurred throughout the United States. This photograph de-picts the arraignment of a Sikh arrested while riding on a Northeast area train the day after the attacks. Sikhism originated in what is now India and Pakistan and many of its male adherents wear a turban and long beard and carry a small, emblematic knife out of view. Because these symbols of their personal religious commitment coincided with the long-standing stereotype of Muslim men in the United States, many found themselves falsely under suspicion by both police officials and their fellow citizens. If this suspicion motivates a search of a Sikh man, police might discover such a knife—as they did in the case pictured above—and have cause for arrest. This is a result of stereotyping.

Stereotyping figured also into the 2006 controversy regarding the publication of cartoons depicting the Prophet Muhammad, first by a Danish newspaper and later by other news outlets. The cartoon at the heart of this scandal—a portrait of the Prophet Muhammad with a bomb as a turban—might appear to be caricature and not a stereotype. If the cartoon portrayed Osama bin Laden it would be taken as such. However, because Western audiences recognize Muhammad as a symbol of Islam, they cannot but read this specific caricature as a claim that all Muslims are essentially violent. When a caricature of an individual becomes a symbol used by outsiders to depict a group, the image passes from caricature to stereotype. If an American political cartoon critiqued Henry Kissinger's political opinions while portraying him with exaggerated bushy hair, unusually large glasses, and a heavier than actual German accent, these would be understood as an acceptable caricature. However, should the cartoon depict him as a Jew with the exaggerations common to anti-Semitic images, it would become an unacceptable stereotype. The same could be said about a caricature as an African American of Dr. Martin Luther King Jr. Significantly, many Americans failed to understand how this could be the case in relation to a Muslim.

STEREOTYPES OF MUSLIMS AS ARABS

If one asks Americans which countries have the most Muslims, all but the most knowledgeable will reply with the names of Middle Eastern nations such as Egypt, Iraq, and Iran. Since Arabs represent the majority population of most of these nations, it is not surprising that one of the most pervasive stereotypes of Muslims is as Arabs. Yet only 20 percent of all Muslims in the world identify themselves as Arabs. The nations with the largest Muslim populations are Indonesia, Pakistan, India, and Bangladesh—very few of whose Muslims consider themselves Arab. Meanwhile, significant numbers of Arabs identify as Christian. Nevertheless, the persistence of the Arab caricature in American stereotypes of Muslims leads to a confusing collapse of difference between the two somewhat overlapping groups. Cartoonists routinely use the *bodies* of Arabs as symbols to caricature Muslims.

For example, this cartoon by Jeff Danziger portrays the predominantly Pashtun Taliban using symbols of Arabs: The men wear Arab kaffiyeh and *thobes*, entirely unlike what most Pashtun men wear. The underlying presumption is that Pashtun Muslims dress as all Muslims dress—as the stereotyped Arab. The cartoonist includes the two figures

Jeff Danziger, 2001. Jeff Danziger, New York Times Syndicate

in burqas and the exhortation "Praise Allah" to emphasize the Muslim quality of the characters.

The stereotype of the Arab as Muslim also relies on expectations of both groups being violent and hypocritical. In Pat Oliphant's cartoon, the Arab is sullen before shrieking his true thoughts on September 11. His words express not simply anti-American sentiment but religious intolerance as well, suggesting that Islamic beliefs inflamed Arab hatred of the United States. Without any labels but "The Arabs," the audience is meant to assume that the caricature represents all Arabs. Also, "the Arabs" are shown to be hypocritical, calling for Saddam Hussein's death but unwilling to do anything about him. Finally, the exaggerated size of the large, beaklike nose serves as a racial symbol of Arab difference. Comparison with the facial features of the woman who questions the Arab draws the reader's attention to the difference between the norm and the Arab.

Of course, the conflation of distinctive physical features with specific behavioral characteristics has occurred before. Despite the differences in their historical contexts, the two cartoons above—one from

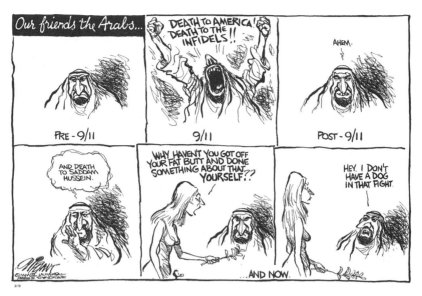

Pat Oliphant, 2003. OLIPHANT 2003 UNIVERSAL PRESS SYNDICATE. Reprinted with permission. All rights reserved.

Vichy France and the other from an American news service—make nearly identical claims. The figure on page 72 is entitled, in French, "The qualities of the Jew." In the several compartments of his brain there exist a propensity to theft, a worship of money, and an unwillingness to serve his country. The Arab figure on page 73, meanwhile, is dominated by vengeance, fanaticism, fantasy, blackmail, and distaste for compromise. In addition to the shared general concept, the figures share a curved, broken nose; facial hair; socially and politically hostile outlooks; and strict, rigid, and narrow thinking. Each ethnic group is affiliated with a common group mindset, and is denied individual, rational thought. Both cartoonists implicitly reaffirm the normality of their target audience by explicitly detailing what supposedly characterizes Jews or Arabs—what makes them different from us.[5]

A common symbol used to depict all Arabs is that of an Arab man who looks unkempt or disheveled. This hints at the "dirty Arab" stereotype not uncommon in both the United States and Europe. In this context, Arabs represent the unhygienic inhabitants of the bleak and waterless desert or of foul and overcrowded cities. Representations of facial hair—unshaven or untidy—most obviously reflect this quality in editorial cartoons.

Of course, it would be an exaggeration to say that all editorial cartoons rely solely on these stereotypes. There are some relatively few examples in which the cartoonist attempts to create sympathy in his or her audience for those who are usually on the receiving end of stereotyped descriptions. One such approach of a more favorable portrayal has

Les qualités du Juif d'apres la méthode de Gall

Emile Courte. Probably 1940 Vichy France.

stereotyped characteristics give way to difference and individuality: in other words, showing a group of Muslims or Arabs who look, dress, or act in heterogeneous ways.

Another approach is more subversive, criticizing the very propensity to stereotype unfairly. This means lampooning not those depicted

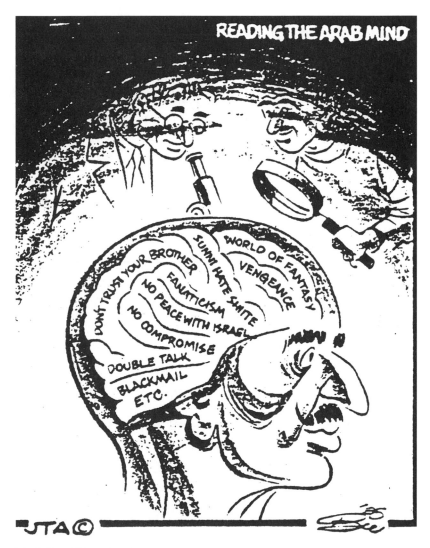

Noah Bee. JTA. c. 1956.

Glenn McCoy, 2002. GLEN MCCOY 2002 Belleville News-Democrat. Reprinted with permission of UNIVERSAL PRESS SYNDICATE. All rights reserved.

Jeff Danziger, 2002. Jeff Danziger, New York Times Syndicate

stereotypically, but rather those who rely on stereotypes, in an attempt to ridicule and undermine the fear-filled universalizations.

USING NEGATIVE STEREOTYPES TO DEFINE AMERICA AS THE GOOD NORM

As already mentioned, stereotypes often implicitly serve to define those who create the stereotype. Through their negative depiction of "them," stereotypes positively define "us" as not like that. Just as when the members of a group are depicted as all having large noses only when it is assumed that this would appear abnormal for the intended audience, so, too, when a person stereotypes one community as dishonest, he insinuates that his own community is generally honest. Chapter 1 described how Middle Eastern Muslims historically have played a role in the negative definition of Western Christians—socially, theologically, and morally. Although the specific dimensions continue to change over time, the same general dynamic exists today.

Overall, these comparisons help Americans affirm their sense of general success in the face not only of the inability of foreign nations to live up to American ideals, but also of various American failures to realize those ideals. In a way, America's enemies help solidify a singular American identity even as they threaten its citizens and interests. They unwittingly do this when U.S. media outlets represent them in such ways that they define what America *is not*. This lends itself to a total alienation of these enemies in order to erase any possibility of commonality or shared quality.

Of course, the key to understanding this enemy is that it is defined not only by those who deliberately aim to be inimical to U.S. goals but

Doug Marlette, 2004. © 2004 Tribune Media Services, Inc.

Table 3.1.   Stereotypes of Muslims and Americans

Muslims	Americans
Two-faced and untrustworthy	Truthful
Regressive or backward	Progressive
Medieval	Modern
Evil	Good

also by an American media that provides the primary means by which most Americans access the representation and interpretation of those antagonists. That media has implicitly implicated Muslim men, and some Muslim women, as inherently enemies of America's "way of life." This implies a unity in lifestyle that Americans must unite to protect. It also presumes that, as table 3.1 illustrates, Muslims by their very nature are inimical to that lifestyle. Hence the oft-repeated calls by media pundits for an "Enlightenment" and "Reformation" by which Muslims can "become modern"; that is, endorse our social choices.

For many American cartoonists, the differences with Muslims stem not only from a superior American character, but also from the fundamental characteristics that define society in the United States, ignoring that nearly 6 million Americans are also Muslim. Danziger's cartoon, below, offers no more insight than a comparison of the supposed sophistication of American baseball to the raw primitiveness of the Afghan game *buzkashi.* He expects his audience to draw for themselves the self-evident conclusions about the different cultures.

The reader notices as well the contrast between the white ballplayer and the dark face of the rider (matching his horse) with his menacing silhouetted eyes.

Interestingly enough, *buzkashi* served as a positive measure of Afghan masculinity and courage in the face of American mendacity and subterfuge in the 1988 movie *Rambo III.* Filmed when Americans celebrated and supported Afghan Islamic militants (*mujahidin*) in their jihad against Soviet invaders, the movie depicts brawny hero John Rambo playing *buzkashi* with equally virile *mujahidin,* some of whom will risk their lives with him in rescuing an American officer abandoned by the U.S. military. The producers went so far as to dedicate the film to "the gallant people of Afghanistan." As the fiasco in Afghanistan—the "Soviet's Vietnam"—evoked memories of America's Vietnam with its bitter experiences of troops feeling betrayed by comfortable politicians as atheistic Communism outlasted U.S. resolve, to some Americans the *mu-*

Can We Learn About Different Cultures from Their Games? For example...

IN THE U.S., THE NATIONAL SPORT REQUIRES A PLAYER TO HIT A BALL THROWN ACROSS A PLATE INSIDE A PRECISION STRIKE ZONE, INSIDE SPECIFIC LINES AND RUN A SERIES OF BASES BEFORE THE BALL IS CAUGHT AND THROWN TO THE RELATIVE BASE, IN WHICH CASE SCORING WILL BE AWARDED ONLY FOR THOSE WHO HAVE REACHED THE FINAL BASE WITHIN THE REQUISITE NUMBER OF OUTS NOTWITHSTANDING...

IN AFGHANISTAN, THE NATIONAL SPORT REQUIRES A MAN TO THROW A BEHEADED GOAT ACROSS A LINE...

Jeff Danziger, 2001. Jeff Danziger, New York Times Syndicate

jahidin represented God-fearing, heroic men whose mettle the the Communists could not defeat. The good feelings toward Afghan Muslims did not last as the *mujahidin* became opportunistic warlords and many ordinary Afghans turned to the Taliban to replace them.

THE DUPLICITOUS MUSLIM: THE SAUDI EXAMPLE

If American cartoonists have taken Arabs as the stereotypical Muslim, since the September 11 attacks they have portrayed Saudi Arabians as the nadir of Muslim duplicity, repression, backwardness, and evil. America's long-standing though troubled relationship with the Kingdom of Saudi Arabia took a particularly awkward turn following the 2001 tragedies. The majority of the hijackers that day originated from Saudi Arabia, as did the plot's presumed mastermind, Osama bin Laden. During the political, economic, and military posturing that followed, President George W. Bush cast the world in Manichaean terms when he informed all non-Americans that "every nation, in every region, now has a decision to make. Either you are with us, or you are with the terrorists."[6] Saudi Arabia did not appear to acquiesce to American needs as readily as expected. The Saudi government failed to adequately implement oil policies intended to ensure inexpensive oil for America and balked at acting as the launch pad for an invasion of Iraq, while wobbly allegations arose of government ties to al Qaeda. Then terrorists in the country itself began targeting Western contractors on which the government and many companies there relied.

True to the nature of stereotypes, many political cartoons collapsed the government, terrorists, and general population in Saudi Arabia into a single depiction that drew on not only physical stereotypes of Arabs but also long-standing assumptions among non-Muslim Europeans and Americans. One such notion is that of deception.

"The Saudi" threatens not only his professed enemies, but those to whom he professes loyalty as well. "The Saudi" says one thing but means another, swears alliance with one group but backs another, and smiles to your face while planting a knife in your back. In other words, Saudis, like other Arabs in many Western depictions, deceive everyone and cannot be trusted.

Pat Oliphant, 2001. OLIPHANT 2001 UNIVERSAL PRESS SYNDICATE. Reprinted with permission. All rights reserved.

OUR ALLY, SAUDI ARABIA, ANNOUNCES AN OPEC PRICE INCREASE

Such a representation in America echoes attitudes dating at least as early as 1780 with the New York premiere of the play *Mahomet, the Imposter* that focused on the Prophet "Mahomet's" manipulations of two innocents for his own nefarious ends. In 1796, Philadelphia audiences also enjoyed a production of the play, which, based on one by Voltaire, had earlier became so popular in England that for more than three decades it was reprinted annually.[7]

Although France and Germany, erstwhile allies of former American foreign policy agendas, even more directly challenged the U.S. government's plans in Iraq, cartoonists, though critical of the two nations, did not resort to the same backstabbing caricature, as demonstrated in the consideration of the depictions of the French at the chapter's end.

MEDIEVAL MUSLIMS AGAINST PROGRESS

Perhaps most central to American perceptions of their own society is the notion of being modern. To be modern is to be as close to the benefits of tomorrow as possible today. As a modern society, America continually puts greater distance between itself and a less enlightened, less developed, and less free past. At its most optimistic, this confidence in modernity relies on a history which arcs from a "primitive" past toward an expected end: a more promising future. The term "progress" defines the distance traveled on this one-way highway of change.

In general, most Americans continue to fundamentally trust that overall conditions are improving, if not for the world, then at least for their country. Moreover, many take as a matter of faith that America moves at the forefront of progress in most, if not all, fields: government, science, education, technology, entertainment, and medicine, among others. Although some may be suspicious of some elements of modernity while others prefer "how things were," Americans in general positively describe themselves and their nation as modern, developed, advanced, and future-oriented, as opposed to those who are medieval, undeveloped, backward, and past-obsessed. Tiny minorities like the Amish and Luddites notwithstanding, even those Americans who espouse "traditional" values commonly conceive their most foundational principles as the apex of a historical timeline.

Traditionalists may pine for a return to the moral conditions of some point in the past, but seldom do they wish to reestablish the entire past. One rarely hears anyone promoting the resurrection of monarchal rule, a rescinding of equal rights for minorities or women, or the abolition of surgical anesthesia. Instead, traditionalists and modernists alike promote democracy, equal rights, and scientific advance as the hallmarks of American progress. Both liberals and conservatives rely heavily on the language of development—change for a better tomorrow—and imagine a common road that all humanity treads, some communities farther along than others, albeit with perhaps differing views of what defines "advanced." Indeed, the language chosen to describe proposed outcomes gives ample testimony to the American faith in a teleology of progress.

This makes for high-wire acts balancing core values with devotion to progress. Although, for instance, conservatives characterize progressive efforts to extend equal rights to gays and lesbians as undermining "traditional values," they may support an American civilizing mission promoting democratic political institutions in an effort to "bring the world into the twenty-first century." Meanwhile many American liberals condemn such projects as dangerously self-congratulatory and ethnocentric, yet nevertheless promote "uplifting" and "empowering" women or "improving" overall human rights in foreign countries through diplomatic and economic pressure to adhere to their own progressive norms. Even Christian fundamentalists, who may decry the corrosive effects of secularism and reflect fondly on an earlier time of supposedly more earnest Christian living, often understand their Christianity as the apex of religious development, a "new" message for the world. In order to disqualify those who claim a newer message, they may explain religions originating since Christianity as either re-embraced relics of the pagan past or (as we have seen in the case of Islam) degenerate forms of Christianity.

Western Europeans and Americans have long taken Arabs, and Muslims in general, as one of the most prominent examples of social, political, moral, and religious backwardness, if not regression. Men like Thomas Jefferson and John Adams, despite their very different political visions, could agree that Islam—synonymous with "Oriental despotism"—obstructed progress because it stood against personal liberty. American writers shared the conclusion with European authors that this despotism resulted from the nature of Islam that engendered bad government and led to public ignorance and social indolence.[8]

At least one important change has occurred in the understanding of Muslim Arab backwardness since the days of the early American republic. Whereas Jefferson and Adams considered Islam as inherently reinforcing the conditions for a nonmodern society, contemporary American commentators often consider Islam as deliberately *anti*-modern. Muslims become defined by their willful rejection of all things modern.[9] Traditional clothing and camel riding are but the external signs of a conscious rejection of the true knowledge, morality, and values of "the modern world." Of course, this simplification disregards the sophisticated commercial and social infrastructure that the Saudis have created that has made it possible for them to export more oil than any other country. Ironically, Saudi Arabia's highly developed oil industry has allowed, until the turn of the millennium, Americans to rely on it, taking for granted its steady flow of crude—unless Saudis and other Arabs decide to withhold or raise its price. In these historical moments, many cartoonists swiftly changed their depictions of Arabs from a backward people to powerful men who brandish their oil business as a threatening weapon (see pp. 119 and 120).

Pat Oliphant, 2004. OLIPHANT 2004 UNIVERSAL PRESS SYNDICATE. Reprinted
with permission. All rights reserved.

Political cartoonists also have used the Taliban of Afghanistan to
demonstrate the anti-modernity of Islam generally. The Taliban's severe
enforcement of religious maxims for personal appearance, behavior, and
gender roles appealed to the worst American expectations for a government motivated by Islam. Its rejection of many Western norms led to
media descriptions of the movement as "medieval" and "regressive,"
driven by its desire to "return to the days of Muhammad," turning away
from the advances of the present that supposedly promise so much for
the future. For some, the Taliban's rejection of Western values could be
equated with the rejection of modernity itself, and this, by default,
meant that they must be anti-American. So, for instance, American media sources often portrayed the severe restrictions imposed on Afghan
television watching and music listening as a rejection of all things Western: entertainment and technology. Several observers wryly noted the
supposed hypocrisy of the same Taliban government employing modern
tanks and aircraft. These conclusions reveal far more about the commentators' worldview than about the Taliban's logic and imply that
modernity comes as a package bound in a Western-designed wrapping

that must be accepted, or rejected, as a whole. Disapproval of any part of the package may be interpreted as not only anti-modern, but anti-Western and/or anti-American as well.

Many American observers project this equation of anti-modernism and anti-Americanism onto all Muslim militants. For instance, President Bush in his 2005 Veterans Day speech described Islamic radicals: "The rest of their grim vision is defined by a warped image of the past—a declaration of war on the idea of progress itself." They must hate America, in this view, because they "despise freedom and progress."[10] There can be no doubting the oppressive rule of the Taliban and the unjustifiable violence inflicted by so many Islamic militants. However, presuming that their motivations derive primarily from anti-Americanism provides little insight into these diverse, complex, and dangerous movements beyond hyperbolic versions of the simplistic conclusion that they are not like us.

It is important to recognize that editorial cartoonists at times also critique certain Americans as against modernity and progress. They have been particularly attentive to the efforts of intelligent design proponents

Bill DeOre, 2001. DE ORE © 2001 Dallas Morning News. Reprinted with permission of UNIVERSAL PRESS SYNDICATE. All rights reserved.

to promote their theories in public school systems, if not to prohibit the teaching of evolution. Significantly enough, however, the cartoons commonly characterize these proponents according to their state or city—Kansas or Dover, Pennsylvania, to name two places where they have had limited success in pursuance of their agenda—rather than as "Christians." Moreover, no single caricature of intelligent design supporters emerges that allows the audience to physically identify them as a stereotype despite their unflattering portrayal as primitive or violent. A cartoon may depict antievolutionists as a blunt-bodied Neolithic caveman, but the audience does not read this as a claim about their actual physique. Cumulatively, political cartoons depict some Christians as anti-modern some of the time *if* they are fundamentalists but most Muslims as anti-modern most of the time *because* they are Muslims.

Tom Toles, 2005. TOLES © 2005 The Washington Post. Reprinted with permission of UNIVERSAL PRESS SYNDICATE. All rights reserved.

EVIL MUSLIMS

The most radical position regarding how Islam deviates from the American norm is its role as a tool of Satan. This perspective is a direct descendant of the medieval Christian allegations regarding Muhammad, and all Muslims, as either the naive puppets or dedicated minions of Satan. Of course, any criminal responsible for the slaughter of thousands of innocents could be portrayed in this manner—as Hitler has been—without any specific theological intent. However, the overwhelming numbers of such portrayals in light of the millennia-old Christian characterizations of Muslims as demonically influenced makes such a conclusion difficult to avoid.

One need only revisit the controversial contrast that General Boykin drew in 2003 between his "real God" and the "idol" god of his Somali Muslim opponent (see chapter 1). Although the Bush administration's support for Boykin did not necessarily signal its agreement with his theology, its unwillingness to reprimand him probably reflected its interest in appeasing the significant number of conservative Christians who

Pat Oliphant, 2001. OLIPHANT 2001 UNIVERSAL PRESS SYNDICATE. Reprinted with permission. All rights reserved.

Tony Auth, 2001. AUTH © 2001 The Philadelphia Inquirer. Reprinted with permission of UNIVERSAL PRESS SYNDICATE. All rights reserved.

Pat Oliphant, 2003. OLIPHANT 2003 UNIVERSAL PRESS SYNDICATE. Reprinted with permission. All rights reserved.

did. At least one cartoonist saw the contradiction between Boykin's self-congratulatory nationalism and triumphalist theology.

AND THEN THERE'S THE FRENCH . . .

In order to address the argument that editorial cartoons necessarily lampoon other peoples and nations in nonflattering terms, it will be useful to consider recent depictions of the French. Many Americans and French people have warily stared at one another across the Atlantic since at least the days of French president Charles de Gaulle, who often steered his nation's foreign and military policies independently of American and NATO concerns. More recently, French antipathy for the rising tide of American cultural hegemony—marked by the arrival of Euro Disney and a proliferation of McDonalds—has heightened the level of mutual disregard. From the American side, the unwillingness of the French, among other governments, to support the American-led invasion of Iraq in 2003 spurred an energetic round of French-bashing by editorialists.

Glenn McCoy, 2005. GLENN MCCOY 2005 Belleville News-Democrat. Reprinted with permission of UNIVERSAL PRESS SYNDICATE. All rights reserved.

Overall, the recent portrayal of the French in editorial cartoons has tended to characterize them as capricious and unreliable, symbolized as white men with pronounced noses, thin and pointy moustaches, and effete demeanor. (As the cartoon on p. 120 demonstrates, this image is not new.) Although such a portrayal has faint parallels with the character of Muslims as irrational and duplicitous and portrayed with large noses, the two clearly stand in stark contrast because of the lack of any racial and religious stereotypes in the French caricatures. Despite the common features in their symbolic depiction, the French do not suffer from the universalized physical image as found in the stereotypes of Muslims. This weakens the overall strength of the impression, since as a symbol the French figure can be no more convincing about some uniform French quality than Uncle Sam can be for Americans, John Bull for the British, or the bear for Russians. The conviction with which many cartoonists depict Muslims physically and personally communicates itself more forcefully to their audience, which understands the difference between symbol, caricature, and stereotype and draws different conclusions from each.

• 4 •

Extreme Muslims and the American Middle Ground

𝒥n December 2001, the National Geographic Society published *The World of Islam*, a volume that included excerpts from articles dealing with Muslim cultures published over nearly a century in the *National Geographic* magazine. The advertisement in the regular magazine caught the overall tenor of the volume when it announced, "Long before our nation focused its attention on the world of Islam, NATIONAL GEOGRAPHIC was there. At a time when most Westerners were forbidden access, our writers and photographers explored the history, culture, and religion, first hand."[1] Projecting the fictional image of a singular and self-isolated world, the Society intended to generate an audience by appealing to American expectations of an Islam associated with withdrawal and secrecy while offering the alluring prospect of revealing tantalizing secrets.

The book underscores these themes of exotic difference in a number of ways. For instance, the volume stands out on a bookshelf because a colorful photo of an exotically masked woman in red acts as a visual exclamation mark above the title printed along the book's spine. Removing the volume from the shelf, one lingers over the cover, with its eerie image of faceless, completely veiled women standing like salt pillars without obvious purpose, direction, or identity. Inside, following an old photograph of the Kaba in Mecca, six double-page photographs precede the foreword: camels below an oil-smoke-darkened sky (Kuwait 1991), the pilgrim-surrounded Kaba at night (Mecca 1966), the shah of Iran facing a Muslim cleric (Iran 1968), a boy leading camels in front of a Palestinian refuge camp (Jordan 1952), Palestinian security forces raiding a Gaza home (Palestine 1996), and Afghan soldiers assembling before a line of tanks (Afghanistan 1993).[2] The themes? Religion, camels, alluring and forbidden women, social turmoil, violence, and American geopolitical interests.

Although the editor in chief of *National Geographic* explains in the foreword that earlier articles unfortunately included "impolitic," "patronizing," and racial insensitivities, he misses at least as important a point. Despite his honesty regarding these embarrassing anachronisms, the editor fails to recognize how essay after essay with image after image in the current volume propound a portrayal of Muslims as eternally exotic and essentially different from the American target audience. The cameras of *National Geographic* appear particularly drawn to the visual and (supposedly) cultural contrasts of kaffiyeh-wearing men flying a modern helicopter or Arabs in a Kentucky Fried Chicken restaurant. Although these images admit the presence among Muslims of these normal components of most Americans' lives, the quaintness and emphasis of the repeated juxtapositions simultaneously reaffirm the absurdity of the connection between the normal and the exotic.

This connection between the normal and the exotic occurs not only in some of the volume's photography, but also in the editor's choice of articles. The Kuwaiti oil wells, shah of Iran, Palestinian refugees, and Afghan soldiers of the photographs that introduce the volume all speak to events when and places where American interests have connected with foreign Muslim lives. Oil reserves, international allies, Israeli security, and the demise of the Soviets after their Afghan fiasco stood as some of the most important U.S. foreign policy concerns throughout the last half of the twentieth century. Meanwhile, more than half of the book's articles deal with that vortex of American political and economic engagements: the Middle East. Although the majority of Muslims live east of Afghanistan, only seven of twenty-seven articles deal with regions there. While *National Geographic* undoubtedly seeks to inform its American readers about regions in the news, it unintentionally reemphasizes to those readers the message that mainstream news reporting repeatedly underscores: the "world of Islam" is defined as inherently in conflict with the interests of Americans.

It would be an exaggeration to imagine that non-Muslim Americans consciously cast Muslims as their antagonists in a deliberate effort to construct an adversary. Instead, as chapter 1 has demonstrated, many of their perceptions have been shaped by the cumulative experience and memories found in the dominant European American culture. These derive from centuries of geopolitical, economic, and theological competition with Mediterranean Muslims. Such experiences have generated assumptions largely left unchallenged due to the lack of wide-scale Western contact with Muslims in a context of political neutrality, or at least equality. These assumptions collide with the norms of mainstream American culture as it has developed historically.

As the last chapter showed, the concept of the norm helps us understand how invisible and unconscious certain oppressive expectations can be, not only among those who suffer them, but especially among those who perpetuate them. Norms are often so pervasive in a community or society that they are not explicitly taught but rather implicitly transmitted from generation to generation. The passing comment of a mother about "those people" or the wrinkled nose of an uncle's disapproval at the sight of "one of the them" represent but one more stone in the foundation of norms by which a child increasingly engages her world. Although those who do not fit the norm are more likely conscious of these expectations, many of them will likely internalize the norm and may even disparage themselves for not "living up" to it.

The invisibility of the norm to those who fit it is well demonstrated with the example of regional accents. To those from a specific area, they speak "normally" while others appear to have an accent. Of course, this norm changes from location to location. A resident of central Connecticut recently explained to one of the authors that only people in the middle of the state had no accent: people on one side sounded like Rhode Islanders and on another like Massachusetts residents. However, the national media has created and reinforced a national norm that transcends regional ones. This is evident in the predominance among national television, radio, and film personalities of a particular type of accent. However one might describe it, this accent makes Southern or New England or Texan accents sound like, well, accents. Most commonly, mainstream television and film features a person speaking with a regional accent only when some stereotypical quality associated with that accent matters for the character: the redneck Southerner, the prim New Englander, or the garrulous Texan. Mainstream media productions, therefore, often communicate a negative impression to the very people they pretend to portray, spurring many to "lose" their accents for the sake of professional and social advancement.

The previous chapter considered how political cartoons often project Muslims and Islam as opposite to and antagonistic of "the American character." This derives from a bipolar worldview common in the consideration of trustworthiness, progress, modernity, freedom, and basic morality. However, another realm of comparison exists that establishes the norm not simply as "good" to whatever might be "bad," but as a moderate middle ground on a spectrum bracketed by extremes. Once again, we notice how the negative representations of a group, culture, or religion often present an insight into the self-perceptions of those making the representation. Americans are not unique in this dynamic: Many, if not most, communities affirm themselves, their ideals, and their values using ethnocentric norms. By examining mainstream U.S. norms, we learn how Americans have relied upon a particular view of Muslims to confirm America's normality.

This chapter will examine five themes through which Americans often have positioned themselves as representing the norm of the middle ground. The common depiction of Muslims as extremists becomes more understandable in light of their association in the minds of Americans with excessive behavior and belief, as table 4.1 shows. Often, Islam represents the extreme of too much: too much religion in the wrong

Table 4.1. Extremes and norms of cultural ideas

	Extreme of Too Little	Norm of the Middle Ground	Extreme of Too Much
Religion and Government	Official atheism	Secularism	Politicized religion
Nationalism	Factionalized	United	None due to transnational Islamism
Men	Effeminate passivity	Proper masculinity	Hyper-masculine rage
Women	Scantily clothed; object of desire	Clothed according to choice	Entirely covered; object of oppression
Morality	Hedonistic	Balanced	Puritanical

places, too much masculinity, or too much female modesty. In some cases, Americans have portrayed individual Muslim cultures as flawed because they suffer from *either* too much of one quality *or* too little of the same. So, for instance, Muslim-majority countries seem *either* crippled from a lack of a unifying nationalist sentiment *or* dangerous due to their promotion of a transnational Islamic community. The chapter will conclude with a brief exploration of the portrayal of Americans in Muslim political cartoons in order to compare themes, caricatures, and symbols.

RELIGION AND GOVERNMENT

It often strikes Americans as odd that religion has played such an important role in the shaping of their national identity since, in various parts of the country, the public discussion of religion makes many uncomfortable. For them, religion belongs to the private realm of the individual conscience, the place of worship, and the home. If made public, religion threatens to unleash dissension and division. Because of this, many of us were warned never to discuss religion or politics at the dinner table, and the unannounced appearance of polite yet proselytizing Mormons or Jehovah's Witnesses at the front door puts some of us on edge.

These sentiments derive from the earliest history of the independent United States that struggled to define itself against its English parent and cope with its multiple religious communities. Thomas Jefferson may have referred to Nature's God in the Declaration of Independence, but he and most of the Constitution signers (almost all of them Freemasons) were uninterested in promoting a specific church. After all, dissident Protestants such as Puritans and Quakers had fled to this side of the Atlantic to escape the persecutions of the state-affiliated Church of England. Meanwhile, Jews and Catholics also had a presence, although they would be denied equal rights until the next century. In addition, the centuries of bloodletting on the European continent motivated (or at least legitimated) in part by Protestant-Catholic antagonisms following the Reformation convinced many eighteenth-century intellectuals like Jefferson that public religion threatened social harmony. Secularism offered an alternative that would be enshrined in the first article of the Bill of Rights: "Congress shall make no law respecting an establishment of religion or prohibiting the free exercise thereof."

Despite these secularist sentiments, a normative Protestant Christianity has deeply influenced the shaping of American mainstream culture and contributed to a paradoxical legacy. If many Americans fear religion pushed on their doorsteps, most fear its absence among their leaders. A 1999 survey showed that only 49 percent of Americans polled said they would be willing to vote for an atheist presidential candidate. Although Jews, women, and blacks can hardly be considered the norm in American politics, 92 percent of respondents replied that they would be willing to vote for a Jewish or female candidate and 95 percent would vote for a black candidate. Even a gay candidate had a better chance of being elected than an atheist.[3]

The sharp debates regarding the presence of the line "one nation, under God" in the Pledge of Allegiance and the presence of "In God We Trust" on every American bill and coin large enough to bear the words are not relics of a quaint but faded religiosity. In fact, it was only in 1954 that Congress added the phrase to the pledge, in an effort to help underline the difference between faithful Americans and godless Soviets. Throughout the Cold War, the atheism of Communism served Americans as one of the primary measures of difference with the United States. Americans came to treat Communism as a type of "perverted faith" that supplanted the proper values of individualism and freedom[4] promoted by true religions. Perhaps this notion informed President Ronald Reagan's famous description of the Soviet Union as an "Evil Empire."

It is also significant that, two decades later, President George W. Bush defined another realm of malevolence when he declared North Korea, Iraq, and Iran an "Axis of Evil." By associating two Muslim-majority nations with the evil of Communist North Korea, Bush suggested that Islam was replacing Communism as the ideology of perennial conflict in America's foreign affairs and perpetual fear in domestic life.

Overall, then, this history of secularism among a religiously active population has inculcated both reservations regarding religion in public life and an aversion to atheism. This has led to a secular norm set between the extremes of overtly religious politics and patently nonbelieving leaders or official atheism.

A series of cartoons by artist Jeff Danziger illustrates the multiple levels of American suspicion regarding Islam. As will become apparent, secular concerns at times faintly mask much older Christian sentiments.

The most common suspicion considers Islam as inherently violent. This cartoon cautions the reader about the militantly religious nature of

The Northern Alliance

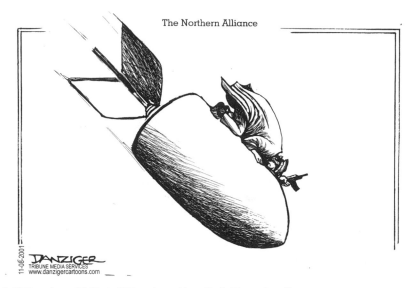

Jeff Danziger, 2001. Jeff Danziger, New York Times Syndicate

America's allies in the war against the Taliban. The image of a prostrate Afghan doing his prescribed prayers atop a falling bomb while clutching a gun demonstrates the failure of secularism among the Muslims of Afghanistan's Northern Alliance and mirrors the superimposed images of Muslim prayer and violence seen in *The Siege*, discussed at the beginning of chapter 3. Whereas personal acts of religious devotion remain safely private in the American secularist ideal, the Afghan (male) Muslim's faith is intrinsically married to violence.

In Danziger's image of Iraq, unkempt, dark fundamentalists pursue their own agendas, equating the innocuous owners of liquor stores and women baring their ankles with the Baathists threatening the social order to the dismay of an American GI. Fundamentalist Islam distorts reality for the unrestrained fanatics warped by it.[5]

At times, a cartoonist attempts to defend Islam from claims regarding its inherent violence and oppression by impugning its "manipulation" by a certain group of Muslims. This places the cartoonist in the odd position of defining which interpretations of the Quran are accurate, Islamic beliefs proper, and forms of practice appropriate. Simultaneously, this dismisses the claims to religious motivations of those who

Jeff Danziger, 2002. Jeff Danziger, New York Times Syndicate

Tony Auth, 2001. AUTH © 2001 The Philadelphia Inquirer. Reprinted with permission of UNIVERSAL PRESS SYNDICATE. All rights reserved.

do not fit the cartoonist's definition of the proper Muslim, relabeling their intentions as merely political, economic, or misogynistic. Overall, then, these cartoons unwittingly reinforce the notion that religion, when true and good, is relegated primarily to a spiritual realm. Those who bring it into other realms "use" it for their own ends, not with appropriately religious intentions.

The American norm of the United States as a God-fearing yet secular nation obscures the historical and political connections between Christianity and government readily apparent to many outsiders. American policies have relied on the acquiescence, if not outright support, of many churches. Christian justifications for enslaving Africans helped perpetuate the slave trade. Many Christian missionaries collaborated with the federal government's efforts to subjugate Native Americans to reservation life. And some Christian nonprofit organizations have blended their government-sponsored roles of administering relief in Afghanistan and Iraq with efforts to proselytize.[6] Despite the long, complicated history of the constitutional battle to define and defend the line between church and state, Christian ideologies, institutions, and language often have infused government policies in the United States. This is not a claim that American secularism has failed, but an observation that its application—like that of any ideology—falls short of its ideals and so blurs the supposedly distinctive line that separates this norm from those to which it is compared.

NATIONALISM

One of the hallmarks of the contemporary world has been the development of the nation. Allegiance to the nation—a collection of individual citizens whose primary attachment is to one another and to their country—began supplanting loyalty to monarchy in eighteenth-century Europe. Over time, governments began to gain legitimacy not from royal claims to divine right but from their ability to represent their nation's citizens. During the next two centuries, many of the directly colonized and imperially dominated peoples of most of the rest of the world would begin imagining themselves as nations. They did so in their attempts to justify self-determination and independence following European and American models. At least as often as not, their borders, and thus their definition of nation, were determined by European imperial powers. This contrasted significantly with American and European patriotic histories, which portrayed each Western nation as coalescing naturally through the mutual recognition of its residents as "a people." As the experiences of Native Americans in the United States, Irish Catholics in Great Britain, and Basques in Spain would demonstrate, the exact bounds of membership to the nation were not always quite so self-evident, open, or accepted. Nevertheless, a different situation existed for those whose encounter with the very notion of nationalism arose from the experience of imperial domination.

For instance, in the wake of the defeat of the Ottoman Empire at the close of World War I, the British seized the three provinces of Basra, Baghdad, and Mosul.[7] From these Ottoman administrative regions, the British created the "nations" of Iraq and Kuwait by drawing borderlines and establishing friendly ruling monarchies according to British eco-

Tom Toles, 2003. TOLES © 2003 The Washington Post. Reprinted with permission of UNIVERSAL PRESS SYNDICATE. All rights reserved.

nomic and political interests and with the cooperation of certain members of the population. The multiethnic and multireligious "people of Iraq" were then left to discover how they would fulfill their foreign-imposed identity. The borders of tiny Kuwait not accidentally contained the lion's share of the region's oil, and its pro-Western dynasty has since ensured the British constant access.

Afghanistan also owes its origins to the British, who in this case established borders not to contain resources but to create a buffer state. The Russian and British empires had played "the Great Game" throughout the nineteenth century in the region between the Northwest Frontier of India and the Russian-controlled Central Asian states. They agreed to borders intended to keep one another at arm's length. The British, meanwhile, deliberately divided the ethnic Pathan tribes of the Hindu Kush Mountains between India and Afghanistan to retard their political consolidation. Contemporary Pakistan inherited this situation when it won independence in 1947, and Pathans continue to often derisively mock their supposedly national government in Islamabad. Few governments have long maintained control over an Afghanistan divided into

Jeff Danziger, 2001. Jeff Danziger, New York Times Syndicate

remote regions by difficult terrain and characterized by widely varying languages, customs, and practices.

The irony of the problems with unity that many of these European-defined nations face is that Europeans and Americans often condemn them for their divisiveness. Taking nationalism as a normative form of social organization and imperially established borders as the natural bounds of a people, Westerners often blame a lack of unity for the failures of some nations—a unity seldom self-understood before the arrival of the Europeans. Since nationalism is a norm of American life, Muslims, most of whom live in areas previously under European domination, appear implicitly unwilling or unable to accede to the sacrifices and compromises required of nationhood as demonstrated in cartoons dealing with the twenty-first-century situation in Afghanistan or Iraq. This factionalism is, at one end of the spectrum of nationalism, extremely deficient.

Glenn McCoy, 2002. GLENN MCCOY 2002 Belleville News-Democrat. Reprinted with permission of UNIVERSAL PRESS SYNDICATE. All rights reserved.

The other extreme that helps define American nationalism as normal is that of transnational Islamism. Although few Muslim leaders have proposed a single transnational Islamic state to replace nations, the concept looms large in the minds of many non-Muslim Westerners. It is perhaps for this reason that American news outlets consistently interpret Osama bin Laden's statements and activities as intending to reestablish the long-extinct caliphate and install himself as caliph. In an address in 2005, Bush argued, "These militants believe that controlling one country will rally the Muslim masses, enabling them to overthrow moderate governments in the region, and establish a radical Islamic empire that reaches from Indonesia to Spain."[8] Little in bin Laden's or al Qaeda's declarations justify such conclusions, however.

Meanwhile, when fears of Islamic terrorism peak, suspicion has occasionally fallen upon Muslim citizens of the United States as alarmists assume that all Muslims pledge allegiance to their religion rather than their nation. The Nation of Islam, often victim of its own intentionally provocative rhetoric, has long garnered such doubts.

In light of this, it is possible for cartoonist Glenn McCoy to depict "DC sniper" John Allen Muhammad and his murderous actions as the product of the Nation of Islam because of his nominal connections with the Nation. Media attention on the intentionally provocative, anti-Jewish, and threatening rhetoric (though the Nation rarely has sponsored actual violence) that used to preach black separatism from white America so dominates non-Muslim perceptions of African American Muslims that most are surprised to learn that merely 10 percent of African American Muslims belong to the Nation. Ninety percent belong to nonseparatist Sunni traditions.

MEN

Overwhelmingly, the depiction of contemporary Muslims is the depiction of Muslim men. These men, as evidenced by most of the cartoons cited in this and earlier chapters, are most often violent and uncouth. Their masculinity is exaggerated in negative directions—toward malevolence and uncontrollability—as opposed to positive directions such as heroism and protectiveness. The abnormality of Muslim masculinity is evident in excessive and unruly facial and body hair. Although many

Muslim men adopt a beard in respectful imitation of the Prophet Muhammad, the stereotype that they are unkempt communicates a lack of restraint.

Historically, American and European depictions of the threatening pose of the hypermasculine Muslim—sometimes drawn as exaggeratedly tall and broad—has contrasted with another image, that of the effeminate Muslim man. As will be seen in the next chapter, the extreme of the effeminate Muslim becomes most apparent in incidences when Muslim-predominant states cautiously negotiate with better armed Western powers.

The depiction of Saddam Hussein transformed during the 2003 standoff between him and the U.S. government. As the possibilities of negotiation evaporated, so did depictions of him as effeminate. Perhaps because the portrayal of Saddam as a threat proved so unconvincing to many, some cartoonists focused instead on the Bush administration's de-

Glenn McCoy, 2003. GLENN MCCOY 2003 Belleville News-Democrat. Reprinted with permission of UNIVERSAL PRESS SYNDICATE. All rights reserved.

Tom Toles, 2004. TOLES © 2004 The Washington Post. Reprinted with permission
of UNIVERSAL PRESS SYNDICATE. All rights reserved.

piction of a nefarious Saddam, nevertheless drawing on menacing masculine caricatures to do so.

These reflections on the two extremes of Muslim masculinity help
explain a particularly disturbing character change in the film *The Siege*,
considered at the beginning of the previous chapter. The film surprises
the audience when a particularly passive character, previously manipulated as an informant by a female FBI agent, suddenly proves himself the
long-sought terrorist mastermind behind a series of explosions by berat-
ing and shooting her. The movie successfully hoodwinks many of its
viewers by playing to the audience's expectations of the effeminate Muslim before shattering these expectations through the character's meta-
morphosis into the other extreme of Muslim masculinity, a change signaled by his abuse of a woman.

WOMEN

One of the defining issues for many Americans regarding the presumed backwardness of Muslims is the position of women. Whereas Muslim women with bare midriffs who peek around diaphanous veils represented an object of exotic titillation for many nineteenth- and early twentieth-century Americans and Europeans, the impact of the feminist movement and increased awareness of gender inequality in the United States and Europe led to an important change. The naive eroticism of the 1960s television program *I Dream of Jeannie* gave way to the accusatory hyperbole of the 1991 film *Not without My Daughter* in which a duplicitous Iranian man—in league with his entire family in Tehran—holds hostage his loving European American wife and their innocent daughter. In the meantime, the Cold War between the "free world" and "enslaved" Soviet Bloc had concluded and a rhetorical shift ensued that

Bill DeOre, 2001. DE ORE © 2001 Dallas Morning News. Reprinted with permission of UNIVERSAL PRESS SYNDICATE. All rights reserved.

repositioned the United States as champion of freedom relative no longer to Communist masters but instead to the fanatic men and subjugated women of the Islamic world.[9]

The totalitarian excesses of the Stalinist state that for so long fueled the justification to interfere in any "Communist-leaning" country's political process now appeared to take similarly threatening form in Islamic politics. Thus, the American invasion of Afghanistan and the overthrow of the Taliban government became the liberation of that country and, more specifically, of its enslaved women.

When the War on Terrorism then targeted Iraq, the dictator Saddam Hussein became the face of tyranny. However, the liberation of women still provided a trump card for the war's apologists as they addressed complaints about the treatment of Iraqis during the American invasion and subsequent occupation of the country, including the infamous revelations from Abu Ghraib prison. This despite the fact that Iraqi women enjoyed one of the highest levels of education and medical care in the Middle East before the 1991 Gulf War, often higher than that found in many of the neighboring countries whom the United States enlisted as allies.[10]

Glenn McCoy, 2004. GLENN MCCOY 2004 Belleville News-Democrat. Reprinted with permission of UNIVERSAL PRESS SYNDICATE. All rights reserved.

Among the many political cartoons depicting Muslims, almost none show Muslim women unless to explicitly remark on their oppressed status. Muslim women seldom figure into representations of Muslims in general. Overall, then, cartoonists appear to practice their own subjugation of Muslim women by denying that they represent Islam at all, although mothers commonly act as the first Islamic teachers for their children. Moreover, cartoonists often ignore the choices many, though certainly not all, Muslim women make in regard to their lives, such as the recent trend among many young women in Egypt, the United States, and other nations to voluntarily adopt the head scarves that their mothers did not wear.[11]

Although an awareness of gender inequality internationally may have motivated concern among editorial cartoonists regarding some "universal plight" among Muslim women, it does not appear that all ensuing critiques have entirely shed the enduring Western titillation with "exotic" and "Oriental" women as either teasingly clad or tantalizingly covered. To be sure, many Muslim women do suffer very real and tragic oppression. The place of honor killing, genital mutilation, and forced marriage in many cultures—though not just Muslim ones—demands attention and concern. However, the assumption that American women live in some ideal normality belies common realities of sexual exploitation and gender oppression that unarguably manifest themselves in the pervasive everyday American tragedies of sexual assault, domestic violence, and eating disorders,[12] not to mention persistently lower pay and promotion rates in the workplace. Perhaps it is the focus on the purported miseries of Muslim women that helps many Americans acquiesce more comfortably to the normality of such local inequalities and domestic crimes. Certainly, heightened awareness of discrimination against women in America has foreclosed romanticizing the genie/Jeannie in a bottle as the Arab/Muslim woman of popular imagination has transformed from the diaphanously dressed object of sexual fantasies to the oppressively veiled object of political liberation.

MORALITY

American cartoonists primarily represent Muslim women in order to project their editorial opinion about Islamic morality. Historically, West-

Jeff Danziger, 2001. Jeff Danziger, New York Times Syndicate

ern views have oscillated between two extreme views of Muslims: as moral militants and as sensually insatiable. Ironically, Muhammad has been portrayed historically as both a puritan for Quranic restrictions on wine drinking and as a hedonist for his marriage to multiple wives. Portrayals of Muslims today continue to gravitate to one or the other of these two extremes. Occasionally, they show both extremes in order to demonstrate Muslim hypocrisy. In one example, the exaggerated puritanical misogyny of the Taliban defeats their attempt to rouse a boy's lust as motivation for violence.

Women remain notably absent in these critiques of Muslim morality, just as in general depictions of Islam. The cartoons focus on them as the objects of male desire and the victims of male power, yet seldom consider Muslim women's perspectives beyond those assumed from afar.

Some cartoons explicitly portray the overall theme of extremism. They express the popular assumption of an inherent extremism among Muslims. For instance, the Oliphant cartoon in the last chapter depicts Saudi religious schools as feigning reform while actually inculcating the rejection of "all democratic and civilizing influences." Other cartoons

Jeff Danziger, 2001. Jeff Danziger, New York Times Syndicate

Chip Bok, 2003. © 2003 Chip Bok. Reprint permission granted by Chip Bok and
Creators Syndicate. All rights reserved.

excoriate the possibility of moderation by either individual Muslim leaders or Islam itself.

CHALLENGING THE NORM

A final measure of the extremes that Muslims represent relative to the American norm appears when people or objects associated with Islam become symbols of abnormality *in situations that do not involve Muslims.* Whereas the previous examples used symbols of Islam and stereotypes of Muslims in negative contrast with American ideals and individuals during encounters between the United States and Muslims, political cartoonists occasionally use symbols of Islam to symbolize unacceptable deviance in general. In this way, various Muslim cultures or individuals, or Islam in general, serve as an absolute marker of abnormality by which to measure divergence from an American norm. And so, an oppressive burqa drapes Ms. Liberty as evidence of an oppressive domestic policy or an attorney general dons the symbolic gear of a mullah.

Tony Auth, 2001. AUTH © 2001 The Philadelphia Inquirer. Reprinted with permission of UNIVERSAL PRESS SYNDICATE. All rights reserved.

Aaron McGruder, 2001. THE BOONDOCKS © 2001 Aaron McGruder. Dist. By UNIVERSAL PRESS SYNDICATE. Reprinted with permission. All rights reserved.

In other instances, however, the cartoonist attempts to draw parallels between excoriated Muslim figures or situations in Muslim cultures and American ones in an effort to challenge the unquestioned acceptance of a specific American norm. In these cases, the cartoonist demonstrates how arguments used to deprecate a Muslim individual or culture may apply to Americans as well. By doing so, they attempt to demonstrate how some American norms prove to be more of an ideal than a political or social reality.

By comparing the idealistic rhetoric of American policy makers regarding Muslim leadership, education, or women's rights to actual conditions on the ground in the United States, these cartoonists turn complaints about Muslim societies into editorial commentary on conditions in the United States itself.

• 5 •

Moments

*W*hat follows is an examination of four distinct moments in the history of the relationship between the United States and Muslim cultures: the Egyptian nationalization of the Suez Canal in 1956, the oil crisis of 1973, the Iranian Revolution and hostage crisis of 1979–1980, and the September 11 attacks with their succeeding events. On each occasion, cartoonists draw on repeating sets of themes, symbols, caricatures, and stereotypes that depict the group in question in a negative, even hostile, fashion. While political cartooning as a whole is an essentially critical art, as discussed in the introduction, these cartoons often go beyond the basic negativity of caricature. Many are, in fact, hostile because the cartoonists, though usually unintentionally, assume the status of being enemies of the groups that they are criticizing.

As we shall see, an evolution occurs in which political figures and movements that happen to be or include Muslims increasingly become identified primarily *as* Muslims. Ultimately, the depiction of these opponents of the United States as Muslim through symbols and stereotypes inherently means to signal to the American audience that they are necessarily antithetical to the audience's values. The symbols and images used serve to associate a wholly negative notion of Islam with these political movements, even when such associations are not appropriate. Moreover, the U.S.-Muslim dichotomy created here necessarily impugns the loyalty of nearly 6 million American Muslims, who must be suspect, first, as Muslims before being embraced, second, as Americans.

The changes and continuities during the fifty years covered by these cartoons reflect the shifting popular concerns toward and increasingly troubled rendering of Muslims and Islam in the mainstream American imagination.

NASSER AND THE SUEZ CANAL: 1956–1958

Egyptian leader Gamal Abdel Nasser was a worrying figure for the U.S. government in the 1950s and 1960s, as the United States had a shaky relationship with Egypt following World War II. U.S. interests were torn between Cold War partner Britain, which wished to maintain military forces in Egypt, and the increasingly nationalistic Egypt, which sought complete national sovereignty. Concern over continued and unfettered access to the strategically vital Suez Canal, which allowed American naval forces rapid transit from the Mediterranean through Egypt to the Red Sea and into both the Persian Gulf and Indian Ocean, further quickened anxieties.

Each side in the dispute initially sought American support. Finally, in 1952, Nasser negotiated the departure of British troops.[1] In late 1955, the United States attempted to assert new influence in the Middle East, as Secretary of State John Foster Dulles proffered financial support for Egypt's nascent Aswan Dam project. However, when Dulles unexpectedly withdrew the offer, Nasser responded by immediately seizing and nationalizing the Suez Canal, which had, in the 1950s, stood under the controlling interest of the British and French. This, in turn, provoked Britain and France to enlist Israel's help and attack Egypt in late 1956.[2] Ultimately, the Eisenhower administration joined the Soviets in pressuring the British, French, and Israelis to abandon their invasion. Nevertheless, the United States remained worried about Nasser.

Throughout the next several years, Nasser espoused a rhetoric of Arab unity and socialism. The Egyptian leader became popular and influential among Arabs in and beyond Egypt after the successful Suez standoff, fashioning and presiding over the short-lived United Arab Republic. He received steady aid from the Soviet Union while allowing an increasing number of Russians into Egypt. U.S. leaders feared that Nasser had opened up the entire Middle East to Soviet influence and that his principle of Arab nationalism might eventually threaten Western access to Middle Eastern oil.[3]

Cartoons of Nasser during this period reflect the American view that Egypt was important only insofar as it had strategic significance in the context of the Cold War. Despite these very contemporary concerns and Nasser's thoroughly modern political outlook, personality, and dress, cartoonists of the period represented him, as well as Egypt as a whole, using the traditional tropes of Arabs, Middle Easterners, and the desert. Furthermore, Nasser and the Middle East were portrayed recurrently as women, or with feminine overtones: This trope connected Nasser to the pervasive European rendering of the Middle East as easily subjugated and Middle Eastern men as feminine and passive. Two cartoons in particular demonstrate these perceptions.

The first cartoon draws explicit attention to the notion of the Middle East as a "vacuum" of political power. This attitude, which

Demonstration on Filling a Vacuum

John R. Stampone. *The Army Times*, 1956.

John Stampone, 1956. Army Times.

understandably frustrated Arab leadership,[4] reflects the U.S. belief that the Arab states stood incapable of exerting meaningful political power. Meanwhile, the pyramid in the first frame acts as a visual clue situating the characters in the land of archaic Egypt, contrasting the Soviet offi-

Cleopatra

Warren King. *Daily News* (New York), 1959.

Warren King, 1959. Daily News (NY).

cer's modern uniform and vacuum cleaner with the landscape's antiquated architecture and the Arab's medieval dress.

The second cartoon uses the same trope of femininity, this time to portray Nasser as the resplendent recipient of fawning Soviet and U.S. attention. The same luscious, sensuous imagery is used, this time with makeup, wine, satin, and jewelry. The caption "Cleopatra" emphatically connects modern Egyptian politics to ancient, somewhat legendary affairs.

Although the guilelessness of the slight female sucked into the Soviets' clutches seems to contrast in terms of agency with the confident seductiveness of Nasser fawned over by the superpowers, in fact they differ little. While the latter image suggests that Nasser can attract the attentions of his foreign admirers, his agency remains obviously feminine and passive, attaining nothing actively, only through the kind offices of the masculine—that is powerful—Soviet Union and United States.

Overall, therefore, three themes dominate the editorial cartoons of this period: Arabs as (1) feminine and passive, (2) archaic, and (3) physically different from Westerners. Other cartoons reflect the prevalence of these themes. One, made by Richard Yardley for the *Baltimore Sun* in 1956, depicts Nasser as a camel. While a smiling woman symbolizing the United Nations pats his injured rear, Uncle Sam waves a patronizing finger at the unhappy figures of Marianne (symbol of France), John Bull (Great Britain), and David Ben-Gurion (Israel's prime minister) while saying, "He'll respond to patience and kindness." Both John Bull and Ben-Gurion hold ruined riding crops that they have apparently broken on the camel's hind. Nasser's caricature as a camel represents not only his obstinacy, but also his association with an archaic culture. Meanwhile, background pyramids, an overhanging palm tree, and a crescent moon and stars further situate the scene in Egypt. We must note that the moon and stars featured prominently on the Egyptian national flag at the time and, therefore, were meant by the cartoonist to symbolize Nasser's Egyptian quality, not his Muslim identity.

Another cartoon from the same year, by Leo Thiele of the *Los Angeles Mirror-News*, takes a different tack to depict Nasser through stereotypes. While a grimacing Uncle Sam and Nikita Khrushchev look on from either side, Nasser sits on an elevated platform in front of a crystal ball that shows Africa and West Asia. These are labeled "Egypt's future policy" and "Mid-East politics." Staring at the ball, Nasser extends an open hand—palm up—in the direction of each figure while saying,

"Cross my palms with silver." The cartoonist's effort of associating Nasser with the charlatan claims of crystal ball readers—whose claims to mystical knowledge are often buttressed by their supposedly exotic origins— is reinforced by Nasser's kaffiyeh, headgear central to American stereo-

Mideast Tableau

Hy Rosen. *The Times-Union* (Albany), 1958.

Hy Rosen, 1958. Reprinted courtesy of Hy Rosen.

types of Arabs yet almost never worn by the Egyptian leader. As with the cartoon on page 114, Nasser's passivity barely hides his effort to swindle money from the superpowers.

The divergence of the cartoon opposite in its portrayal of Nasser from the earlier examples is the exception that proves the rule. Compared to the feminine and/or manipulative Nasser in the previous cartoons, the masculinity of this Nasser is exaggerated. The cartoonist has liberally dabbed the Egyptian leader's legs, forearms, chest, and chin with hair stubble to magnify a brutishness also made visible in both his conniving grimace and the array of weapons at his side. Editorial cartoonists of this period use both extremes of masculinity, as described in chapter 4, to portray Nasser as aberrant from the "normal" man: either mockingly faux-feminine or menacingly hypermasculine. Association with ancient Egypt would also be a central theme to this and other period portrayals.

It should be noted that the physical differences in portrayals of Arabs in this period focus primarily on clothing and that Muslim identity did not seem to matter. Whereas the caricature of Soviet premier Nikita Khrushchev wears a business suit, the symbolic Uncle Sam dons his emblematic striped pants and tails, and other international leaders or symbols wear Western clothes, none of the images of Nasser portray him in the business suits that he favored. Instead he wears an ancient Egyptian wrap, a diaphanous dress, and an Arab kaffiyeh. In yet another image, he is a camel in all but his recognizable facial profile. Despite their use of this unusual clothing, these cartoons do not represent Arabs as *bodily* different from others. Most notable, however, is the absence of references to Islam or stereotypes of Muslims in these images. It would not appear that Nasser's Muslim identity mattered in the perceptions of these cartoonists so much as his identification with Egypt, an identification defined by its ancient past. However, a stereotype presuming racial and religious difference would soon dominate portrayals of Arabs and, later, other Muslims.[5]

OIL CRISIS: 1973–1974

On October 17, 1973, during the Arab-Israeli Yom Kippur War (also called the Ramadan War or October War), several of the Arab oil-producing states—notably Saudi Arabia—imposed an oil embargo on the United States, Japan, and certain European countries. Ostensibly this was in response to American support for Israel in the war. The use of oil as an economic, and therefore political, bargaining chip succeeded, and the price of oil in the United States skyrocketed. Prices immediately rose 70 percent, and eventually reached 400 percent of their original price in the United States over the course of the six-month embargo. This concerted strategy on behalf of the Arab oil states came as a surprise to most Americans and the U.S. government. The Nixon administration and many others assumed that any effort at Arab unity would fail, and so they could dismiss Arab threats of using oil for political leverage.[6] In fact, Henry Kissinger remarked derisively about the Saudi foreign minister: He's "a good little boy," so "we don't expect an oil cutoff in the next few days."[7]

The energy crisis in the United States provoked a sense of anger toward the Arab oil states. Media accounts and editorials angrily condemned the Arab use of oil as a weapon.[8] Some feared that an economically hobbled America would be vulnerable to proliferating purchases of businesses and real estate by Arabs.[9] Political cartoons prodigiously manifested this resentment through pernicious stereotypes of Arab physical features, aggressive countenance, and moral character. During this period, cartoonists represented Arabs as undifferentiated in their stereotyped qualities as scheming and money mongering, qualities already portrayed in caricatures of Nasser two decades earlier. Now, however, Arabs were not acting passively. Instead, the united effort of some to institute an embargo had apparently put them in control of the economic fate of the United States. Underlying the majority of the cartoons during this period, we see that the deep-rooted Euro-American association of Islam with violence, nascent during Nasser's rule and the Suez Crisis, is highlighted, providing a backdrop for understanding of this modern, economically driven situation.

Caricatures of this period rely upon several potent symbols that would become standard in the portrayal of Arabs, and Muslims generally, from then on. Throughout, the use of the kaffiyeh immediately informs the reader that the subject is an Arab. The caricatures commonly wear facial hair, angry smirks, droopy eyes, and heavy eyebrows, and their noses cast beaklike and broken from their faces.

These two cartoons mark the perceived contrast between Arab and European physiognomy and aggression. The Arab's nose and facial hair

BIG GUN

Bill Mauldin, 1973. Copyright 1973 by Bill Mauldin. Reprinted courtesy of the William Mauldin Estate.

are as prominent as his threatened or actual violence. In both cases, kaffiyeh-adorned Arabs wield oil or oil prices as weapons to intimidate or assault unarmed and dismayed Western nations. Furthermore, the type of weapon the second cartoonist chooses is symbolic: an exaggerated scimitar—the symbol of Muslim Arab martial difference originally used to

Neal von Hedemann, 1974.

Neal von Hedemann, 1974. King Features Syndicate.

distinguish them from Christian European Crusaders but suggesting here Arab backwardness. The presence of a scimitar to depict a situation that involved no actual violence against industrial nations offers a historical foreshadowing of its prominence in depictions of later, armed confrontations between the United States and Arab or Muslim states or organizations, as noted in chapter 2.

The overall tenor of many of the cartoons from this period emphasizes an Arab will to power. One cartoon by Bill Mauldin, published at the height of the embargo in December 1973, makes no overt reference to the oil crisis. With its image of a contentedly smiling Arab playing with the globe at the end of a string, it makes no effort to convince its audience of a fact that it assumes its audience will already know: The embargo derives from Arab avarice. The cartoonist suggests that the Arab-Israeli conflict, the oil embargo, and global manipulation are all of a piece.

If these editorial cartoons played to the stereotype of Arabs being medieval and aggressive in contrast with Americans and Europeans as modern and sensible, other cartoons would emphasize Arab extremism.

The following two cartoons depict the sensuality and gluttony often associated with Muslim male hedonism.

The cartoon below lays bare in a surprisingly obvious way the historical roots of these stereotypes. Oliphant's composition appears to owe its framing, perspective, and scale entirely to a nineteenth-century Orientalist painting by Jean-Léon Gérome entitled *Le Charmeur des serpentes* (The Snake Charmer).[10] Instead of the painting's depiction of a turbaned group of Arab warriors reclining against walls decorated with Islamic calligraphy and enjoying the view of a naked boy enwrapped by a phallic python, the cartoon portrays kaffiyeh-wearing Arabs reclining against a wall of oil barrels and intoxicated by their indulgent pastime, as though the Arab producers were the oversatiated consumers of oil. Although the homoeroticism and pedophilia of the original image has not been rendered, the portrayal of a leisurely, indulgent, and sensuous male existence remains. Note how the speaker initiates the Venezuelan—Venezuela being the major non-Arab OPEC state—into the stupefying Arab ways of appreciating life.

If the cartoons of the oil embargo period rely on the extremes of either rage or indulgence to stereotype Arabs, they predictably do so by

Pat Oliphant. *The Denver Post*, 1973.

Pat Oliphant, 1973. OLIPHANT ©1973 UNIVERSAL PRESS SYNDICATE.
Reprinted with permission. All rights reserved.

portraying them only as male. As previously discussed, these extremes inherently assume an oppressed or victimized female. The harem—that
obsessive feature of so much Western attention from the medieval period
through to the modern—commonly symbolizes this other extreme. Pat
Oliphant demonstrates this with his rapacious male personification of
OPEC dominating his "harem" of oil-importing nations, portrayed as
repressed women. This gendered personification presents a commentary
on both the political situation and the situation of women in societies in
which harem culture is supposedly characteristic.

A final example demonstrates how, from the 1970s onward, a presumed Muslim character increasingly would become central to the depiction of Arabs. Replicating one of the postures in Muslim formal
prayer, the kneeling position of this caricature of Saudi Arabia's King
Faisal, combined with his altered nose, implies that his religious suppli-
cation is indistinguishable from his financial covetousness. Meanwhile,
the stereotyped distinctiveness of his nose, so clearly familar from the
anti-Semiticism of the first half of the century, has been obscenely transformed into a symbol of not only Arab otherness but Arab greed as well.

The cartoons of the 1973 OPEC oil crisis consistently employ certain symbols and stereotyped features. Physically, the Arabs are given
large misshapen noses, facial hair, furry eyebrows, and generally vile and

David Levine, 1974. © David Levine/New York Review of Books.

sly countenances. They strictly wear matching kaffiyehs. They are greedy, conniving, scheming, and violent, and they control the future of the United States. As Melani McAlister points out, "This was the beginning of what would soon become a staple of American pop cultural images: the greedy oil sheiks, with their hands on America's collective throat."[11] In many instances, the caricatures appear to have drawn unconsciously on anti-Semitic stereotypes that were used—and occasionally still are—to communicate similar qualities about Jews. Although there are only some overt allusions to Islam in this period, the references to violence, oppressiveness, and a certain indulgent lifestyle certainly draw on latent associations between Arab and Muslim, associations that American responses to events in the near future would recall and reinforce.

IRANIAN REVOLUTION AND HOSTAGE CRISIS: 1979–1980

As described briefly in chapter 2, the Iranian Revolution of 1979, as well as the depth of anti-American feeling that accompanied it, came as a shock to many Americans.[12] Although a broad spectrum of Iranian political interests—from the leftist Fedayeen to the rightist mullahs—and common citizens rose up against the U.S.-backed government of Mohammed Reza Shah Pahlavi, ultimately Ayatollah Ruhollah Khomeini, a Shiite social reformer and government critic, would become the political and religious leader of Iran. When the deposed shah was granted sanctuary by President Jimmy Carter in the United States, all sides supporting the Iranian revolution were furious. The shah represented for many Iranians an oppressive regime first established by a coup. Engineered by British intelligence and the CIA, the 1953 conspiracy replaced the democratically elected prime minister with the shah's father. Incensed by yet another American intrusion into their domestic politics and in order to force the return of the shah, young Iranian revolutionaries took over the U.S. embassy in Tehran, taking more than seventy American hostages in the process.[13]

During the 444 days of the crisis, the hostages in Iran became a frustrating and humiliating symbol of America's inability to act. Nightly television reports on the situation brought the hostages, and their individual stories, into American homes. Accompanying these reports and updated daily, a count measured the number of days the crisis dragged on. American news media made the revolution an American event, portraying Khomeini as "obdurate, powerful, and deeply angry at the United States," and presenting the popular revolt as a defeat for the United States, rather than as a complex political, economic, and religious movement.[14] In his survey of print journalism and rhetoric during the Iran hostage crisis, R. E. Dowling observed several descriptive categories consistently employed by the media to describe Khomeini: old and sick, mentally deficient, morally deficient, spiritually bankrupt, politically opportunist, and an incompetent leader.[15]

The political cartoons of this period contributed to this impression. They present Khomeini and the Islamic revolutionaries of Iran as crazy, backward, and violent. For the first time in twentieth-century America, Islam—as a religious phenomenon—stands at the forefront of depictions of a political challenge by people who happen to Muslim. Many Americans assume Islamic ideologies to be the motivating force behind all Iranian revolutionaries, when they are, in fact, not. Whereas earlier in the century Middle Eastern antagonists were Arabs who *happened* to be Muslim, those in this period are seen as antagonistic *because* they are Muslims, and are Muslim in their entire character. This portrayal indicts not only Iranian Muslims, but Islam itself.

Many contemporary cartoons of this period depict Khomeini's Islam as the worst kind of religion. If the atheism of the Soviet Union represented one extreme on the spectrum of religion and politics, the overtly religious language and leadership of postrevolutionary Iran stand at the other extreme. Not only do cartoons of this period make farce of the religious tenor of Iranian political rhetoric, they also imply a primitiveness and violence to the religion itself. In the context of American social memory, the marriage of politics and religion appears a dangerous step backward toward the intolerant tyranny of medieval government. Whether portrayed as the master of a witches' coven or as inscrutable and scimitar wielding, Khomeini appears as the nightmarish enemy of normative American secularism and a hazard to his own people.

Jeff MacNelly, 1979. ©1979 Richmond Times-Dispatch

Mike Peters, 1979. © Mike Peters. Reprint permission granted by Mike Peters and Creators Syndicate. All rights reserved.

Many Americans assume that all political systems should adhere to a single progressive track that mirrors the West's own history—from states legitimated by religion to the supposed secularism of the modern United States. This outlook immediately disapproves of the replacement of the shah's authoritarian regime—no matter how oppressive—by the ayatollah's theocratic democracy. Certainly, Khomeini's regime was repressive, rejecting many Western and liberal institutions that existed under the shah. However, cartoonists in their representations totalized these rejections as a turning back of the clock, presuming that when Islam plays a public role this must imply a total rejection of all that modernity offers. In other words, Islam fosters backwardness when allowed into the public sphere.

Again, we find the familiar pattern that the gendered image of the fanatical Muslim man is countered with a portrayal of the oppressed Muslim woman. Despite the important role of Iranian women in the revolution, their place in American editorial cartoons seems relegated to one of fashion and slavery. They seldom appear in any depictions of their nation's successful mass movement despite the prominence of their participation. In the image on page 128, not only does the burqa (uncommon in Iran, where women more commonly wear chadors that cover their hair but show their faces) hide the woman from Tehran, it makes

Hy Rosen, 1979. Reprinted courtesy of Hy Rosen.

Jeff MacNelly, 1979. ©1979 Richmond Times-Dispatch

Mike Keefe, 1979. Mike Keefe, The Denver Post.

her fat, short, and deformed. Ironically, the fact that the artist portrays the Iranian woman's oppression by showing how she is unable to appear beautiful relative to stick-limbed Westerners reflects the very fixation on female attractiveness that Muslim women in a variety of cultures associate with Western societies. Many—living in and out of the West—have sought to escape what they describe as sexual exploitation by voluntarily adopting various forms of more conservative dress.[16] This does not ameliorate the restrictions that forced many Iranian women into chadors against their will. It does, however, emphasize that Iranian women demonstrated more agency than portrayed in political cartoons, which often reflect American expectations more than foreign realities.

It is, of course, important to recognize that some cartoonists could critique the stereotypes that seized so many in the United States during this period, even as the newscasters' tallies of the days of America's indignity steadily grew larger. Berkeley Breathed, for one, captured the unfortunate mixture of ignorance and anger that led to the harassment at this time of so many people—many not even Iranian—on the mistaken assumption that their appearance, accent, or religion identified them as Iranian.

The Academia Waltz by Berkeley Breathed

1979 Berkeley Breathed

Berkeley Breathed, 1979. © 1979, Berkeley Breathed. Distributed by the Washington Post Writers Group. Reprinted with Permission.

Cartoons of this period portray Khomeini and the Iranian Revolution as backward, violent, crazy, and irrational, in part because of their association with Islam. The cartoonists present Islam as a powerful, fearful influence, and Khomeini as the evil symbol of that force. Significantly, the cartoons grappling with the Iranian Revolution do not rely on the physiological stereotypes used to portray Arabs. Although Khomeini's beard and garb may have served in caricatures of him, cartoonists do not depict him using stereotypical Arab features. Moreover, while their work borrows certain Muslim-associated themes (e.g., violence) and symbols (e.g., the scimitar), the cartoonists do not use Arab-related symbols to depict Iranians, despite the fact that a 1980 poll showed that 70 percent of Americans thought that Iran was an Arab country.[17] (In general, Iranians do not view themselves as Arab, and their language is not a Semitic one as is Arabic.) However, the differentiation of Muslims demonstrated in this period would frequently fail at the turn of the century as artists too often collapsed Arab, Muslim, Islam, terrorist, and oppressor into one image.

9/11, REPRISAL ON AFGHANISTAN, AND THE INVASION OF IRAQ

The entirely unanticipated horrors of the September 11 attacks succeeded in their goals of terrorizing many complacent Americans and rallying some disaffected Muslims. However, these criminal acts originally

brought unprecedented global sympathy and support for the United States—from Muslims and non-Muslims alike. Although a small number of Muslims, among others, around the world cheered at America's supposed humbling, they remained a minuscule minority at the time.

Editorial cartoonists joined other Americans with forceful patriotic demonstrations. As outlined in chapter 2, these commonly relied on the dual depiction of a victimized America symbolized by a dazed and battered Ms. Liberty and a vengeful America in the person of an angry and resolute Uncle Sam.

Understandably, editorial cartoonists portrayed the hijackers responsible for the murder of thousands in the most sinister manner. However, the particular symbols and stereotypes they employed suggest much more than the diabolical character of these individuals, reaching into stock portrayals of Muslims and Islam.

Although the widely published photographs of the terrorists showed the world uniformly clean-cut men in Western apparel, many

Glenn McCoy, 2001. GLEN MCCOY 2001 Belleville News-Democrat. Reprinted with permission of UNIVERSAL PRESS SYNDICATE. All rights reserved.

cartoonists relied on a standard stereotype of a militant Muslim for their caricatures. In this example, besides the bandolier and time bomb suggesting this hijacker's cartoonlike belligerence, his head wrap and scraggly beard immediately distances him from the American audience as a Muslim man identifiable through stereotypes. Indeed, despite the published and broadcast condemnations of these unjustifiable crimes by Muslim leaders around the globe,[18] American news outlets often focused on Muslim celebrations of the attack.

Unsurprisingly, many cartoonists correlate the hijackers and masterminds like Osama bin Laden with hellishness. However, the deep persistence of this motif, coupled with other stereotypes about Muslims, suggests that they more than accidentally echo medieval formulations that Islam is inherently evil, as described in chapter 3.

Many cartoonists express the notion of Islam as flawed, prone to violence, and essentially oppressive. Following the attacks, the United States roused from its shock. First it took to dismantling the Taliban

Pat Oliphant, 2001. OLIPHANT 2001 UNIVERSAL PRESS SYNDICATE. Reprinted with permission. All rights reserved.

Tony Auth, 2001. AUTH © 2001 The Philadelphia Inquirer. Reprinted with permission of UNIVERSAL PRESS SYNDICATE. All rights reserved.

leadership in Afghanistan that had sheltered bin Laden and his al Qaeda camps. Then it led an assembly of nations to invade Iraq on the incorrect premises that Saddam Hussein's oppressive and brutal regime stood in league with al Qaeda and developed weapons of mass destruction. Throughout these foreign engagements and in response to other world events, a great many editorial cartoons emphasized the retarded, repressive, and renegade nature of Islam. When President George W. Bush in 2002 defined Iran, Iraq, and North Korea as an "Axis of Evil," many in his American audience understood the implied relationship. The total lack of political association between these three nations and their governments at the time did not eclipse the easily appreciable evil leanings of two identifiably "Muslim" nations and a Communist one. The reference to them as an axis intended to allude to the irredeemable evil of the tripartite Axis of World War II: Germany, Italy, and Japan.

The Axis powers of the 1940s could be—and were—defeated, democratized, and transformed into allies. However, the contemporary threat in Afghanistan, Iraq, and, potentially, every Muslim nation arises

12/19 (week of 12/17 vacation sub)

Ben Sargent, 2001. SARGENT © 2001 Austin American-Statesman. Reprinted with permission of UNIVERSAL PRESS SYNDICATE. All rights reserved.

from what many Americans consider an irredeemable feature of those countries that prohibits constructive change: Islam. The danger comes from an inherently extreme religious ideology presumed to be antagonistic to modern education, science, nationhood, and democracy, and characterized instead by backwardness, intolerance, extremism, and violence. Even at a time when local school boards around the United States debate the inclusion in public education of intelligent design curricula based on Christian theology, education systems in Muslim-predominant nations become suspect and excoriated when Islamic learning is included, as demonstrated in the cartoons in chapter 3.

The image on the previous page by Ben Sargent assembles a familiar set of symbols used by cartoonists to personify terrorism as a primitive, rag-headed Muslim horse or camel rider wielding his scimitar. Post-9/11 portrayals of the hijackers as technological naïfs pummeling the modern world with their medieval weapons stand in stark contrast with the nightmarish images—burned into the individual and collective memories of all Americans—of Muslim terrorists piloting advanced airliners with devastating precision into vulnerable buildings. Only the fixity of Islamic backwardness in the popular imagination can possibly account for the coexistence of these images in the media.

Jeff MacNelly, 1990. © 1990 Tribune Media Services, Inc.

A cartoon from the first Gulf War demonstrates that this ingrained notion of Muslim backwardness did not diminish following the Iranian Revolution. Despite the fact that the Iraqi military at that time fielded a considerable force of modern armored vehicles and combat aircraft and that Hussein's Baathist government could hardly be described as Islamic, the cartoonist visually depicts the enemy as a primitive horse rider and verbally demonstrates his Islamic character. The raised scimitar underlines the connection between the two qualities.

The perception of the questionable character of Islam also coincides with Western fixations on specific gender issues. So, for instance, a focus in the media on the seventy-two virgins supposedly promised to male Islamic martyrs met American expectations regarding the hedonism of Muslim men. This religiously promoted sexual bonanza simultaneously impeached the religion that promoted it—despite the rarity of its actual belief—and the martyrs ostensibly motivated by it.

The exaggerated masculinity of Muslim men lends itself to an irrational violence not only among those defying U.S. policy aims, but even among America's Muslim allies. A Jeff Danziger cartoon from 2001 portrays a wide-eyed Uncle Sam attempting to retain control of two manic

Jeff Danziger, 2001. Jeff Danziger, New York Times Syndicate.

members of the Northern Alliance using leashes. While Uncle Sam un-
convincingly assures someone on his cell phone that he's in charge, one
of the Pashtun-dressed men yells, "ON TO PAKISTAN!!" and the
other, "KILL! KILL!"

It is interesting to note that such representations most often appear
in the context of the failing War on Terror, mocking the hypermas-
culinity of the apparently unending supply of Muslim warriors/terror-
ists/separatists. However, in situations of American victory, the defeated
Muslim males slide to the other extreme as their masculinity gives way
to feminization.

Dana Summers, 2005. ©2005 Tribune Media Services, Inc.

**Bill DeOre, 2001. DE ORE © 2001 Dallas
Morning News. Reprinted with permission
of UNIVERSAL PRESS SYNDICATE. All
rights reserved.**

Glenn McCoy, 2003. GLENN MCCOY 2003 Belleville News-Democrat. Reprinted with permission of UNIVERSAL PRESS SYNDICATE. All rights reserved.

Meanwhile, the allegations of Arab and Muslim double-dealing and faithlessness remained unmitigated throughout this period in relation to "moderate" Arab states. Egypt (personified by President Hosni Mubarak), Saudi Arabia, and Turkey had for decades served as the closest Middle Eastern allies to the United States outside of Israel, but when their governments refused to support American plans to invade Iraq, cartoonists portrayed them as traitors. Although Germany and France also failed to live up to the expectations of the Bush administration, cartoonists seldom depicted them as vociferously as these predominantly Muslim countries. In 2003 cartoon, Bill DeOre drew a deviously smiling Lucy pulling away the football from the hapless Charlie Brown to depict Turkey's decision not to support the U.S.-led invasion of Iraq.

All of this is not to ignore the critical engagements of political cartoonists with American foreign policy and cultural and religious stereotypes. Some, like Garry Trudeau's Doonesbury strip, seek to satirize sensationalized media portrayals of Muslims and Islam. Trudeau especially

Tony Auth, 2001. AUTH © 2001 The Philadelphia Inquirer. Reprinted with permission of UNIVERSAL PRESS SYNDICATE. All rights reserved.

Pat Oliphant, 2003. OLIPHANT 2003 UNIVERSAL PRESS SYNDICATE. Reprinted
with permission. All rights reserved.

Garry Trudeau, 2002. DOONESBURY © 2002 G. B. Trudeau. Reprinted with permission of UNIVERSAL PRESS SYNDICATE. All rights reserved.

succeeds when he uses his stock group of familiar characters to interface
with individuals whose mundane concerns (such as saving treats for one's
younger brother) intersect with current events. Doonesbury aims at
more than irony in such depictions, intending instead to demonstrate
that despite their differences members of demonized groups share a basic humanity with the reader.

Ben Sargent, 2003. SARGENT © 2003 Austin American-Statesman. Reprinted
with permission of UNIVERSAL PRESS SYNDICATE. All rights reserved.

Tony Auth, 2003. AUTH © 2003 The Philadelphia Inquirer. Reprinted with permission of UNIVERSAL PRESS SYNDICATE. All rights reserved.

Report Says 1700 Civilians Killed in US Attack on Baghdad

Jeff Danziger, 2003. Jeff Danziger, New York Times Syndicate.

Meanwhile, singular examples of editorial cartoons have challenged stated American policy interests and motivations while simultaneously transcending Arab and Muslim stereotypes in their portrayals of Iraqis and Afghans. These have prompted their American audience to perceive these people as not reducible to an ethnic or religious identity.

Yet other cartoonists have seen beyond American secular norms and recognized the ways in which particular government programs—like the faith-based (read: Christian) initiatives that have long served to distribute U.S. foreign aid—have a decidedly religious bent.

Unfortunately, such examples remain in the minority, while many more depictions rely on an understood homogeneity among Muslims. This may be expressed with a visual lack of differentiation or with a resignation to the inscrutability of Muslims and their cultures.

Tom Toles, 2001. TOLES © 2001 The Washington Post. Reprinted with permission of UNIVERSAL PRESS SYNDICATE. All rights reserved.

Such inscrutability makes understanding impossible. When understanding fails, so does communication, and, with it, the chance to find common cause and a shared humanity.

It would be optimistic to say that the increasingly discrete and decreasingly stereotyped cartoons dealing with the war in Iraq following its first few years arise from greater awareness of the need for this understanding. However, this trend may equally result from the need of Americans to discover Muslims worth the cost of their soldiers' lives, demonstrating once more that popular American portrayals of Muslims and Islam offer far more insight into American self-understanding than into Muslim cultures.

Conclusion: Common Denominators versus Essential Difference

$\mathcal{I}$n response to the tragedies of September 11th, the television series *The West Wing* diverged from its usual practice with a special episode. Previously the show, which depicted the lives of a fictitious president and his staff, did not include any Muslim characters unless the plot required a representative of an Arab government, and usually then when that government sponsored terrorism. In the special episode, a technical expert working in the White House comes under the sharp-edged suspicion of the chief of staff who harshly interrogates him, already convinced that the man, a Muslim, conspires with terrorists. When proven wrong, the chief of staff proffers an awkward apology as the expression of the screenwriter's moral lesson that we must be careful about stereotypes. Indeed, as this, the last scene in the episode, fades to black, the Vietnam-era Buffalo Springfield song "For What It's Worth" emphasizes the point with its cautionary lyrics of fear instilled and sides taken. Yet, these undoubtedly well-intentioned gestures notwithstanding, the silence of all the previous episodes in which no character has a Muslim identity, despite the quite visibly Catholic and Jewish identities of two of the main characters, speaks far louder. Once again, the silence maintained by the media regarding Muslims until they are perceived as a threat means that Muslims become visible as people only when they represent threats *as Muslims*, and thus, they exist only as Muslims. This reinforces the negative view of Muslims and enduringly excludes them from the perceived American norm.

This anecdote demonstrates the larger argument of this book: Media outlets broadcast a series of repetitive messages regarding Muslims and Islam that mutually reinforce negative views among American non-Muslims through both what they say, write, or show *and* what they do not. Because Muslims as Muslims do not fit into the American norm, popular representations do not depict them as part of everyday American life. Instead, they appear when the need arises to include a Muslim, and then, shorn of all other identities—like American or football fan or salesperson—they stand as only Muslim men or Muslim women, with the built-in expectations about what this means. And because they exist only as Muslims, they are assumed to live as a single community, acting as a single body responsible for every member. Their concerns tend to be editorialized as those of a people apart from the West whose essential qualities put them at odds with the West, especially in terms of human rights. In other words, Muslim concerns arise from and reinforce a difference from those of the West. This is implicit in even the terms of the debate: Muslims versus the West, religion versus secularism.

Paradoxically, even American Muslims who successfully enter mainstream U.S. life often attract negative media attention aroused by Islamophobia. For example, in 2006 while interviewing Keith Ellison, the first Muslim elected to the House of Representatives, a CNN anchor focused first on Ellison's Muslim identity. As a prelude for engaging him in his stand, shared by most of his Democrat colleagues, against the Iraq War, the anchor said to Ellison, "No offense, and I know Muslims. I like Muslims. And I have to tell you, I have been nervous about this interview with you, because what I feel like saying is, 'Sir, prove to me that you are not working with our enemies.'"[1] Not only do many members of the media characterize Muslims as Muslims to the exclusion of any other aspect of their identity—like being American—but some in the media seek to benefit from those who would manipulate Islamophobia for political advantage. A few months after the CNN interview, both Fox News and the *New York Post* reported that Senator Barack Obama, a Democratic contender in the next presidential election, had attended a madrasah and was hiding his upbringing as a Muslim despite his self-representation as a Christian. CNN and a variety of newspapers quickly debunked the story as originating from a conservative online journal without any named author or source.[2] Although some media outlets may resist the temptation, many others feed their audience's anxieties about Muslims, perpetuating notions of radical difference for the sake of ratings that surge through a sensationalism born at the intersection of fear and anger.

The controversy over the cartoons depicting the Prophet Muhammad published in Danish and other European newspapers sadly illustrates this conclusion. Almost immediately the Western media spun the issue as one fitting into a history of two irreconcilable worldviews locked in a zero-sum contest of survival: the inalienable freedoms of the West and the imperious orthodoxy of Islam. Any concession by either side represents a step backward.

Yet the conflict could easily have been portrayed as similar to previous debates in the West regarding the depiction of minority communities in popular media. Why the sudden amnesia about the vicious depictions of Jews in political cartoons from Nazi Germany? Why the rarity of comparison to global Christian outrage regarding the release of the cinematic portrayal of Jesus in Martin Scorsese's *The Last Temptation of Christ* in 1989 or similar protest against the satiric critique of Christianity in *Monty Python's Life of Brian* in 1979? Scorsese's film led not only to bomb threats at theaters in the United States but also bans in many nations. In another parallel, at least nine European nations today outlaw the public denial of the Holocaust or the diminishment of its actuality.[3] Instead of placing the controversy among these similar issues, most of the American media immediately depicted the debate as yet another emblem of Muslim difference and Islamic threat.

In fact, no freedom exists without limit. Hate speech laws mete out punishment for certain types of invective accompanying violence. Unsubstantiated smears denigrating an individual's reputation are grounds for suit. Society defends co-workers from unwelcome verbal advances through sexual harassment codes.

Of course, as an element of news reporting and an expression of editorial opinion, political cartoons deserve special protection. They intend to provoke, usually relying on caricature, symbolism, and simplicity to express, in few or no words, their message. Throughout modern history and across the globe, such cartoons have enraged their targets by influencing their audiences.

However, various groups have long maintained a strict surveillance and engaged in practiced protests over editorial cartoons, having recognized that their powers of persuasion may run in damaging directions. The long list of stereotyped features (both physical and behavioral) associated with historically oppressed groups such as African Americans, Jews, women, Latinos, Catholics, and gays and lesbians (to name but a few) need no rehearsal here: They have been publicly protested and successfully minimized, though not entirely eliminated. Outrage has been the starting point of these groups' efforts to demonstrate that caricatures passing as common knowledge sometimes camouflage, often unconsciously, malicious stereotypes.

The reduction of the Prophet Muhammad to a symbol of terrorism reduced all Muslims to the stereotype of the terrorist. Muslim protest against the Danish cartoons escalated—entwined regionally with divergent political issues—from an outrage against the disparagement not only of them, but of the exemplar of Islam, too. Most Muslims understand Muhammad as the perfect manifestation of Islam's ideals, the founder of the first Islamic society, and the model of proper human behavior. Any depiction of him as a militant not only denigrates this beloved figure but also stains the character of Islam and, by default, impugns their own dignity, already sensitive to Western disparagements and suspicions during centuries of European imperial domination followed by today's American hegemony.

The violence that has occasionally accompanied the protests of this cartoon cannot be condoned. And critical inquiry must be protected. However, there must be a realistic recognition that none of the freedoms we embrace stands alone; rather, each balances against other freedoms in an ever-contested, dynamic tension. Westerners must also acknowledge that these particular cartoons exist not in isolation, but as the latest manifestation of more than a millennium of Western portrayals of Muhammad as representing the antithesis of truth, godliness, morality, and freedom.

That the same newspaper that originally ran the cartoon rejected cartoons satirizing Jesus because it would "provoke an outcry" demonstrates that its editors recognize that rights must be balanced with responsibility—or, at least, with the newspaper's economic interests. So why does the *potential* protest of Christians prompt an acceptable act of self-censorship while the *actual* protest of Muslims represents reprehensible censorship? The answer to this question rests in the all too readily anticipated conflict between "Islamic intolerance" and "Western truth"—an imagined tension perennially renewed yet a millennium old. The Associated Press gave voice to this view when it reported, "So far the West and Islamic nations remain at loggerheads over fundamental, but conflicting cultural imperatives—the Western democratic assertion of a right to free speech and press freedom, versus the Islamic dictum against any representation of the Prophet Muhammad."[4] Such an over-simplification erases the hundreds of years of cultural, political, military, and economic interactions between a wide variety of societies erroneously lumped together as "Western" or "Islamic." The editors recognized the potential for caricatures of Jesus to be as inflammatory as the ones of Muhammad. The difference is not in the response but in the decision as to which expected outrage the newspaper sought to inflame and which it sought to avoid.

Despite the span of five decades and the differences in location, cause, and actor, the events we have considered in the last century include the same set of basic images. Physiologically, the stereotype of the Semitic figure persists throughout these events, with the exception of the non-Arab Iranian Revolution. The ancient tropes of Islam, represented through specific symbols, are continually applied to all things Middle Eastern: violence, irrationality, deserts, corrupt leadership, and sexuality. During the middle of the twentieth century, Americans generally did not yet view happenings in the Middle East as being influenced by Islam; rather, the threat was conceived in terms of the Cold War, and as the danger of Pan-Arab nationalism. But cartoonists nonetheless drew on images they associated with Islam, having inherited these conceptions from the Orientalist artistic legacy of the United States, as well as from impressions—perhaps latent—of Islam understood from European history. During and after the Iranian Revolution, Americans finally recognized Islam as a dominant factor—that is, as a motivating force behind certain popular movements. But for political cartoonists, this shift in thought did not complicate their work: They already implicitly utilized Islam as a unifying, explanatory factor in cartoons about the Middle East. Throughout periods of conflict with the perceived Muslim world, Islam provided an understanding of why we were at odds. Historian Christina Michelmore nicely sums up the situation: "As an explanation, Islam eliminates space and time, political complications, ideological incompatibilities. Ageless Islam hates the west."[5]

Of course, such reflections lead us to wonder how issues of representing others play out in non-American Muslim perspectives of Americans. Certainly the defining images in the U.S. media of Muslim attitudes toward Americans—Iranians holding the hostages of "the Great Satan," the 757 poised just meters from the remaining World Trade Center tower, the Palestinian boy shooting his machine gun in celebration at the news—seem conclusive. They are not.

This book could not hope to examine fully American and non-American portrayals of one another. Such a project requires far more expertise in the diverse historical, linguistic, and cultural backgrounds of Muslims than the authors command. As stated in the introduction, this imbalance is hardly a failure of American cartoons alone. It would be tempting to rely on U.S. websites dedicated to malicious imaging by Muslims, but these selectively choose the most egregious examples from

Corky Trinidad, 2002. Reprinted courtesy of Corky Trinidad and the Honolulu Star-Bulletin.

the start. It may appear helpful to examine websites that publish cartoonists from around the world, but these might edit for offensive content. To reach any conclusion beyond the most tenuous requires definitive research in indigenous languages and actual contexts. Moreover, the diversity among Muslim cultures must be taken into account. We fervently hope someone will take up this challenge.

How can the trends in America be addressed? Obviously, the essential simplicity of caricaturing in editorial cartoons will not change. However, other aspects easily can be altered, and some cartoonists already have made the effort. First, the fact could be recognized that Muslims take part in every aspect of American life as businesspeople, college students, government officials, and neighbors. Their inclusion in images depicting Americans *acting as Americans* would help reinforce this notion in the popular mind. Second, cartoons can use caricatures showing personal traits—thus emphasizing individual differences—instead of stereotypes of group sameness. Third, certain symbols by which cartoonists

Chip Bok, 2004. © 2004 Chip Bok. Reprint permission granted by Chip Bok and Creators Syndicate. All rights reserved.

represent Islam should be abandoned since they represent a chauvinistic cultural memory rather than an accurate social reality. Finally, the multiplicity of Muslim perspectives need not be depicted as inherently resulting in violence, the diversity of Muslim cultures can be considered without concluding that Muslims essentially are divisive, and the pronouncements of vociferous Muslim ideologues should not be taken as though they represent Islam as a whole. In other words, Muslims could be portrayed with the same nuance that most cartoonists bring to their depictions of Christians.

Further and more in-depth research would certainly contribute to the effort of demonstrating these claims. Clearly the present volume exhausts neither the topic of Islamophobia nor its portrayal in political cartoons. A historically broader and historiographically more detailed examination of political cartoons would consider examples from several other periods, such as World War II, the Afghan resistance to the Soviet invasion, and the first Gulf War. Moreover, a critical engagement with the cartoons could be situated profitably in the larger context of the newspaper and its editorial pages, where the reader commonly sees them. Letters of response could offer important insights into reader reception.[6]

Other efforts could be made to broaden the research done here. For one thing, a more exhaustive survey comparing how American political

©2005 Lexington Herald-Leader

Joel Pett, 2005. © 2005 Joel Pett. All rights reserved.

cartoonists depict various national, racial, religious, and ethnic groups would be most helpful. Also, the work of Muslim cartoonists in the United States and abroad could be examined.

In the wake of Islamic-inspired terrorism in the West, many observers have questioned the wisdom of inviting Muslims to settle here. We hope that this book adds to a conversation that wonders not only about the unwillingness of some of these migrants to acculturate to the American norm but also about the inability of many non-Muslim Westerners to imagine Muslims being not just "them," but "us." No matter what ideologues on either side say, the large population of American Muslims, to which the increasing number of conversions to Islam in the United States adds annually, means that America is already part of the Muslim world. They have already become us. The question remains whether messages in the media will enable the many Muslims who simply wish to lead their lives untroubled among their non-Muslim neighbors to feel included or not. If alienation will be the rule, then can we not expect Muslims domestically—as so many have abroad—to turn back on non-Muslim Americans the same question asked among so many of us: "Why do they hate us?"

Notes

INTRODUCTION

1. Charles Ferro, "The Last Word: Flemming Rose: Igniting More Than Debate," *Newsweek International*, February 13, 2006, http://www.msnbc.msn.com/id/11179140/site/newsweek/from/RL.1/ (accessed February 18, 2006).

2. Anthony Shadid and Kevin Sullivan, "Anatomy of the Cartoon Protest Movement; Opposing Certainties Widen Gap between West and Muslim World," *Washington Post*, February 16, 2006. A01.

3. Mark MacKinnon, "Word of Mouth Helping to Feed Muslim Rage over Cartoons," *Globe and Mail* (Canada), February 10, 2006. A10.

4. Alan Cowell, "West Beginning to See Wide Islamic Protests as Sign of Deep Gulf," *New York Times*, February 9, 2006, A1.

5. John E. Woods, "Imagining and Stereotyping Islam," in *Muslims in America: Opportunities and Challenges*, ed. Asad Husain, John E. Woods, and Javeed Akhter (Chicago: International Strategy and Policy Institute, 1996), 45.

6. For examples of such testimony, see Fadwa El Guindi, *Veil: Modesty, Privacy and Resistance (Dress, Body, Culture)* (New York: Berg, 1999); Sherifa Zuhur, *Revealing Reveiling: Islamist Gender Ideology in Contemporary Egypt* (Albany: SUNY Press, 1992); Elizabeth Warnock Fernea, *In Search of Islamic Feminism: One Woman's Global Journey* (New York: Doubleday, 1998).

7. For negative depictions in literature, see Edward Said, *Orientalism* (New York: Vintage Books, 1979); on film see Jack Shaheen, *Reel Bad Arabs: How Hollywood Vilifies a People* (New York: Olive Branch Press, 2003); and on the media in general see Melani McAlister, *Epic Encounters: Culture, Media, and U.S. Interests in the Middle East, 1945–2000* (Berkeley and Los Angeles: University of California Press, 2001).

8. "Muslims Must Speak Out," *New London (CT) Day*, July 20, 2005, A6.

9. Stephen Hess and Milton Kaplan, *The Ungentlemanly Art: A History of American Political Cartoons*, rev. ed. (New York: Macmillan, 1975), 13.

10. Christina Michelmore, "Old Pictures in New Frames: Images of Islam and Muslims in Post World War II American Political Cartoons," *Journal of American & Comparative Cultures* 23 (Winter 2000): 37.

11. Ethan Bronner, e-mail correspondence with the authors, November 17, 2003. Mr. Bronner is assistant editorial page editor of the *New York Times*, and in this quote paraphrased the view of Gail Collins, editorial page editor of the *Times*.

12. Walt Kelly, "Pogo Looks at the Abominable Snowman," in *The Funnies: An American Idiom*, ed. David Manning White and Robert Abel (New York: Free Press of Glencoe, 1963), 290.

CHAPTER 1

1. From http://www.msnbc.com/news/980841.asp (accessed October 21, 2003).

2. The outcry did prompt General Boykin to claim that his comments had been misinterpreted. He said, "My comments to Osman Otto in Mogadishu were not referencing his worship of Allah but his worship of money and power; idolatry," Boykin said. "He was a corrupt man, not a follower of Islam." Matt Kelley, "General Apologizes to Those Offended by His Religious Comments," Associated Press, October 17, 2003.

3. Frederick Denny, *An Introduction to Islam* (New York: Macmillan, 2005), 144.

4. Musa ibn Ishaq, *The Life of Muhammad*, trans A. Guillaume (Karachi: Oxford University Press, 1987), 683.

5. Titus Burckhardt, *Mirror of the Intellect: Essays on Traditional Science & Sacred Art*, trans. William Stoddart. (Albany: SUNY Press, 1987), 96.

6. Dante Alighieri, *The Divine Comedy*, trans. Henry Francis Cary (New York: Thomas Y. Crowell & Company, 1897), 154–55.

7. Denny, *Introduction to Islam*, 144.

8. Albert Hourani, *Islam in European Thought* (Cambridge: Cambridge University Press, 1991), 9.

9. Elizabeth Siberry, "Images of the Crusades in the Nineteenth and Twentieth Centuries," in *The Oxford Illustrated History of the Crusades*, ed. Jonathan Riley-Smith (New York: Oxford University Press, 1995), 385.

10. Narcus Bull, "Origins," in *The Oxford Illustrated History of the Crusades*, ed. Jonathan Riley-Smith (New York: Oxford University Press, 1995), 31.

11. Robert E. Van Voorst, *Readings in Christianity* (New York: Wadsworth, 1997), 121.

12. Robert M. Seltzer, *Jewish People, Jewish Thought: The Jewish Experience in History* (New York: Macmillan, 1980), 355.

13. Jonathan Riley-Smith, "The Crusading Movement and Historians," in *The Oxford Illustrated History of the Crusades*, ed. Jonathan Riley-Smth (New York: Oxford University Press, 1995), 4.

14. W. Montgomery Watt, *The Influence of Islam on Medieval Europe* (Edinburgh: Edinburgh University Press, 1972), 46.

15. Europeans came to know the Iberian Muslims as Moors. The term derives from Mauritania, an ancient Roman province in North Africa from which the Muslims who invaded the Iberian Peninsula originated.

16. Watt, *Influence of Islam*, 46.

17. Norman Housley, "The Crusading Movement: 1274–1700," in *The Oxford Illustrated History of the Crusades*, ed. Jonathan Riley-Smth (New York: Oxford University Press, 1995), 268–69.

18. Christopher Columbus, *The Libro De Las Profecias of Christopher Columbus: An en face edition*, trans. Delno West & August Kling (Gainesville: University of Florida Press, 1992), 63.

19. This global perspective on Western imperialism and hegemony derives from the work of the preeminent world historian of Islam Marshall Hodgson, particularly the third volume of his authoritative *The Venture of Islam* (Chicago: University of Chicago Press, 1974).

20. Syed Ahmad Khan, "The Importance of Western Education," in *Sources of Indian Tradition*, vol. 2, *Modern India and Pakistan*, ed. Stephen Hay (New York: Columbia University Press, 1988), 189.

21. William Muir, quoted in Hourani, *Islam in European Thought*, 19.

22. Michael A. Gomez, *Exchanging Our Country Marks: The Transformation of African Identities in the Colonial and Antebellum South* (Chapel Hill: University of North Carolina Press, 1998), 67.

23. Allan D. Austin, *African Muslims in Antebellum America: Transatlantic Stories and Spiritual Struggles* (New York: Routledge, 1997), 12.

24. Sylviane A. Diouf, *Servants of Allah: African Muslims Enslaved in the Americas* (New York: New York University Press, 1998), 17–18.

25. Diouf, *Servants of Allah*, 149.

26. Diouf, *Servants of Allah*, 54.

27. Austin, *African Muslims*, 13.

28. Diouf, *Servants of Allah*, 99–100.

29. Gomez, *Exchanging Our Country Marks*, 68, 82.

30. As quoted in Austin, *African Muslims*, 79; Mark Twain, "American Travel Letters, Series 2 [the last letter]," *Alta California*, August 1, 1869.

31. Robert J. Allison, *The Crescent Obscured: The United States and the Muslim World, 1776–1815* (New York: Oxford University Press, 1996), 35.

32. Allison, *The Crescent Obscured*, 40.

33. Allison, *The Crescent Obscured*, 46.

34. Allison, *The Crescent Obscured*, 59.

35. Allison, *The Crescent Obscured*, 10.

36. Francis Scott Key, "Song," in *Poems of the Late Francis Scott Key, Esq.* (New York: Robert Carter & Brothers, 1857), 34–36.

37. Allison, *The Crescent Obscured*, 33.

38. Holly Edwards, "A Million and One Nights: Orientalism in America, 1870–1930," in *Noble Dreams, Wicked Pleasures: Orientalism in America, 1870–1930*, ed. Holly Edwards (Princeton, NJ: Princeton University Press, 2000), 39–40.

39. Edwards, "A Million and One Nights," 43, 50.

40. Shaheen, *Reel Bad Arabs*, 424–25.

41. Frank Ninkovich, *The United States and Imperialism* (Oxford: Blackwell, 2001), 32.

42. Ninkovich, *The United States and Imperialism*, 52.

43. McAlister, *Epic Encounters*, 37–38.

44. Jane I. Smith, *Islam in America* (New York: Columbia University Press, 1999), 52.

45. McAlister, *Epic Encounters*, 49.

46. McAlister, *Epic Encounters*, 52.

47. McAlister, *Epic Encounters*, 81.

48. Charles Tripp, *A History of Iraq* (Cambridge: Cambridge University Press, 2002), 31.

CHAPTER 2

1. In a paradox typical, too, of derogatory names used by the majority (such as "nigger"), oppressed minorities have often appropriated the symbols of their subjugation and converted them into symbols of their pride, as many lesbians and gays have taken the Nazi-derived symbol as their own.

2. Helmut Nickel, "A Crusader's Sword: Concerning the Effigy of Jean d'Alluye," *Metropolitan Museum Journal* 26 (1991): 123.

3. The authoritative *Oxford English Dictionary* fails to find an adequate etymology for the term. One of the more plausible origins is the Persian *shamshir*, which refers to a sword with a sharply curved blade first produced in seventeenth-century Persia. A. R. Zaky, "Medieval Arab Arms," in *Islamic Arms and Armour*, ed. Robert Elgood (London: Scholar Press, 1979), 211.

4. George S. Patton Jr., "The Form and Use of the Saber," *Cavalry Journal*, March 1913.

5. For the history of the Marine sword, please see the sitemap at the USMC website: http://www.marines.com/page/usmc.jsp?flashRedirect=true (accessed November 12, 2005).

6. Erika Bourguignon, "Vienna and Memory: Anthropology and Experience," *Ethos* 24, no. 2 (June 1996): 379.

7. Interestingly, Conrad used this same technique in a 1970 cartoon depicting a Southeast Asian city bombed by Americans. Foreign Policy Association, *A Cartoon History of United States Foreign Policy, 1776–1976* (New York: William Morrow, 1975), 147.

8. For a fully articulated argument for and demonstration of this, see Leila Ahmed's *A Border Passage: From Cairo to America—A Woman's Journey* (New York: Penguin, 2000), 93–134.

CHAPTER 3

1. Randall P. Harrison, *The Cartoon: Communication to the Quick* (Beverly Hills: SAGE, 1981), 54.

2. William Feaver, introduction to *Masters of Caricature*, ed. Ann Gould (New York: Knopf, 1981), 10–12. It may not always be clear whether the features of a caricature originally become associated with a specific animal because of a perception of the nature of the animal or because of a perceived likeness between the animal and a vilified group of people.

3. Ronald Stockton, "Ethnic Archetypes and the Arab Image," in *The Development of Arab-American Identity*, ed. Ernest McCarus (Ann Arbor: University of Michigan Press, 1994), 119.

4. Walter Lippmann, *Public Opinion*, new material ed. (New Brunswick, NJ: Transaction, 1991), 31, 89.

5. Of more than passing interest, the American caricature was published by JTA, the self-described "global news service of the Jewish people" (http://www.jta.org). Jeremy Zwelling argues that it is not unusual for Jews, like other groups that have suffered oppression, to turn the themes of their oppressors against other opponents once they have obtained a position of security (personal conversation, May 3, 2006). See Amnon Rubinstein's *The Zionist Dream Revisited: From Herzl to Gush Emunim and Back* (New York: Schocken, 1984).

6. George W. Bush, Address to a Joint Session of Congress and the American People, Office of the Press Secretary, September 20, 2001, http://www.whitehouse.gov/news/releases/2001/09/20010920–8.html (accessed April 21, 2006).

7. Allison, *The Crescent Obscured*, 43–45.

8. Allison, *The Crescent Obscured*, 46, 53.

9. Mahmood Mamdani, *Good Muslim, Bad Muslim: America, the Cold War, and the Roots of Terror* (New York: Pantheon, 2004), 17–19.

10. President Commemorates Veterans Day, Discusses War on Terror," November 11, 2005. http://www.whitehouse.gov/news/releases/2005/11/20051111–1.html (accessed November 13, 2005).

CHAPTER 4

1. *National Geographic*, February 2002.

2. Don Belt, ed. *The World of Islam* (Washington, DC: National Geographic, 2001), 1–13.

3. Peter Steinfels, "Beliefs," *New York Times*, March 24, 2001, B6.

4. McAlister, *Epic Encounters*, 52.

5. The use of the term "fundamentalist" represents yet another imposition of Christian concepts on Islam. An early twentieth-century American Christian revivalist movement originated the term to describe their quest to return to Christianity's fundamental beliefs. Since the latter part of that century, common usage has ascribed a negative connotation to the term, suggesting a religious impulse prone to narrow-mindedness and dogmatism.

6. See Erica Bornstein, *The Spirit of Development: Protestant NGOs, Morality, and Economics in Zimbabwe* (Stanford, CA: Stanford University Press, 2005).

7. Tripp, *History of Iraq*, 31.

8. George W. Bush, Speech delivered at Elmendorf Air Force Base in Anchorage, Alaska, November 14, 2005, http://www.whitehouse.gov/news/releases/2005/11/20051114–3.html (accessed May 16, 2006).

9. McAlister, *Epic Encounters*, 51–53.

10. Human Rights Watch, "Background on Women's Status in Iraq Prior to the Fall of the Saddam Hussein Government," November 2003, http://www.hrw.org/backgrounder/wrd/iraq-women.htm (accessed May 7, 2006).

11. For a personal account of the role of elder women as Islamic teachers, see Ahmed's *A Border Passage*. For a study of Egyptian women choosing to wear head scarves and face covering, see Zuhur, *Revealing Reveiling*.

12. For instance, the National Center for Injury Prevention and Control, part of the Centers for Disease Control and Prevention, reports that more than 5 million incidents of women victimized by intimate partners occur in the United States each year. This leads to almost 2 million injuries and nearly thirteen hundred deaths annually. Overall, almost 30 percent of all American women have been physically or psychologically assaulted or raped by someone they knew well at one time in their lives. CDC, "Intimate Partner Violence: Overview," http://www.cdc.gov/ncipc/factsheets/ipvfacts.htm (accessed March 17, 2006).

CHAPTER 5

1. Peter Hahn, "National Security Concerns in U.S. Policy toward Egypt, 1949–1956," in *The Middle East and the United States: A Historical and Political Reassessment*, ed. David W. Lesch (Boulder, CO: Westview Press, 2003), 91.
2. Stephen E. Ambrose and Douglas G. Brinkley, *Rise to Globalism: American Foreign Policy Since 1938* (New York: Penguin, 1997), 153–57.
3. McAlister, *Epic Encounters*, 81.
4. Ambrose and Brinkley, *Rise to Globalism*, 158.
5. We thank Bruce Masters for this insight.
6. Ambrose and Brinkley, *Rise to Globalism*, 263.
7. Higgins, "In Quest for Energy Security," A6.
8. McAlister, *Epic Encounters*, 135.
9. John E. Woods, "Imagining and Stereotyping Islam," in *Muslims in America: Opportunities and Challenges*, ed. Asad Husain, John E. Woods, and Javeed Akhter (Chicago: International Strategy and Policy Institute, 1996), 67.
10. Coincidentally (and accurately) enough, the painting provides the cover art for Edward Said's *Orientalism*.
11. McAlister, *Epic Encounters*, 136.
12. Ambrose and Brinkley, *Rise to Globalism*, 293–98.
13. Ambrose and Brinkley, *Rise to Globalism*, 298.
14. Edward Said, *Covering Islam*, rev. ed. (New York: Vintage, 1997), 6.
15. Ralph Edward Dowling, "Rhetorical Vision and Print Journalism: Reporting the Iran Hostage Crisis in America" (PhD diss., University of Denver, 1984), ii. Dowling contrasts this with the portrayal of Carter, whose descriptions included good leader, restrained, Christian, humanitarian, concerned for the hostages, politically motivated, and then finally, a bad leader.
16. For scholarship on this trend, see El Guindi, *Veil*.
17. Shelly Slade, "The Image of the Arab in America, Analysis of a Poll on American Attitudes." *Middle East Journal* 35 (Spring 1981): 148.
18. For samples of these Muslim condemnations, see the bibliography.

CONCLUSION

1. Noam Cohan, "With Brash Hosts, Headline News Finds More Viewers in Prime Time," *New York Times*, December 4, 2006, C1.
2. "CNN Debunks False Report about Obama," January 23, 2007, http://www.cnn.com/2007/POLITICS/01/22/obama.madrassa/index.html (accessed February 11, 2007).

3. Matthew Schofield, "Historian Gets Prison for Denying the Holocaust," *Boston Globe*, February 21, 2006, http://www.boston.com/news/world/europe/articles/2006/02/21/historian_gets_prison_for_denying_the_holocaust/ (accessed February 23, 2006).

4. Njadvara Musa, "At Least 15 Die in Nigeria Cartoon Protest," Associated Press, February 19, 2006.

5. Michelmore, "Old Pictures in New Frames," 47.

6. We thank Vijay Pinch for this suggestion.

Note on Terms and Names

$\mathcal{T}$he difficulties of rendering into English names and terms originating in non-English languages are numerous. This has been particularly true of words that derive from Arabic, a language both written in scripts that do not commonly depict short vowels and pronounced with variation by its myriad speakers. The same is somewhat true for Persian. Therefore, the name Muhammad—most commonly written in Arabic using only the consonants m, h, m, d—has variously been reproduced in English as Mohammad, Mohammed, Muhammad, and Muhammed. Historically, those with an incomplete understanding of Arabic have also rendered the name as Mahomet and Mohamed. Meanwhile, some authors have attempted to reflect long vowels by doubling them in English, writing Kaaba for Kaba, for instance. Finally, some terms have worked their way into the English language with an everyday version such as Koran, instead of the more accurate transliteration of Quran.

Because this book is intended for a general audience, it represents non-English words or names following scholarly convention except where this causes unnecessary confusion. Therefore, transliteration markings used to denote Qur'ān are omitted and Quran preferred instead.

Finally, as a product of empirical scholarship, this book makes no claims about the "true" definition of Islam or the "proper" behavior and beliefs of Muslims. The large scope of its investigation requires that the volume necessarily generalize about the religion and its adherents while avoiding definitive claims about either. The authors shun universalizations by using modifiers like "many" and "most" rather than "all" in describing even the most common concepts and practices. More than one billion people across myriad cultures and countries identify themselves as Muslim. The only thing more astonishing than their diversity as Muslims is the common significance of the term "Islam"—variously defined in meaning and requirement—in so many of their lives. We take this as a nonpartisan starting point in the description of Muslims and their cultures: their self-description as part of Islam.

Glossary

Although this book avoids the use of diacritics as unnecessary for the general audience, diacritics and renderings of terms in their original are provided here for interested readers. Arabic proper names and place names are given in their original.

Abraham *ibrāhīm*; patriarch and prophet considered a friend of God because of his total devotion to God as demonstrated by his sacrifice of son Ishmael.

Allah *allāh*; "The One" or the only god.

burqa *burqaʿ*; a full-length covering some Muslim women wear to completely clothe themselves.

Ishmael *ismāʿīl*; celebrated as the son of Abraham and Hagar who the former nearly sacrificed in obedience to Allah.

Islam *islām*; "to submit."

hajj *ḥajj*; the annual pilgrimage to Mecca and Medina to visit the sites associated with the prophets.

hijab *ḥijāb*; a scarf that some Muslim women use to cover part of their head; a variety of forms exist.

Jerusalem *al-quds*; site of Muhammad's ascent to Paradise and, therefore, third most revered site for many Muslims.

Jesus *ʿīsā*; one of the book-delivering prophets, he revealed the Gospels to humanity; ascended into heaven after death and will return to announce Judgment Day.

jihad	*jihād*; "righteous struggle" that can be against evil in oneself or external enemies.
Kaba	*ka'ba*; the mammoth, cube-shaped building (from which the English term *cube* derives) considered as the first mosque, built by either Adam or Abraham and rebuilt by Noah; almost all Muslims face in the direction of the Kaba while praying *salat*.
kaffiyeh	*kaffiyah*; an Arab headdress for men.
Mecca	*makka*; the birthplace of the prophet Muhammad, the site of the Kaba, and the most revered place among most Muslims.
Medina	*madîna*; adopted home of the prophet Muhammad and the second most revered place among most Muslims.
Muslim	*muslim*; "one who submits."
Muhammad	*muḥammad*; 570?–634 CE; considered the final prophet to whom Allah sent the final revelation, the Quran, and the leader of the first Muslim society.
People of the Book	*ahl al-kitāb*; the Quran's designation for the Jews, Christians, Muslims, and Sabians (whose identity remains uncertain), communities to whom revealed books have been sent.
Quran	*qur'ān*; the final revelation of Allah, transmitted to humanity through Muhammad.
salat	*ṣalāt*; the formal, five-times-daily prayer performed by most Muslims, comprised of a series of standing, bowing, kneeling, and prostrate positions.

Bibliography

ISLAM AND MUSLIM CULTURES

Abdo, Geneive. *Mecca and Main Street: Muslim Life in America after 9/11.* New York: Oxford University Press, 2006.

Ahmed, Leila. *A Border Passage: From Cairo to America—A Woman's Journey.* New York: Penguin, 2000.

———. *Women and Gender in Islam.* New Haven, CT: Yale University Press, 1992.

Ayoub, Mahmoud M. *The Qur'an and Its Interpreters.* Volume 1. Albany: SUNY Press, 1984.

Burckhardt, Titus. *Mirror of the Intellect: Essays on Traditional Science & Sacred Art.* Translated by William Stoddart. Albany: SUNY Press, 1987.

Denny, Frederick. *An Introduction to Islam.* New York: Macmillan, 2005.

Elgood, Robert, ed. *Islamic Arms and Armour.* London: Scholar Press, 1979.

El Guindi, Fadwa. *Veil: Modesty, Privacy and Resistance (Dress, Body, Culture).* New York: Berg, 1999.

Ernst, Carl W. *Following Muhammad: Rethinking Islam in the Contemporary World.* Chapel Hill: University of North Carolina Press, 2003.

Esposito, John, ed. *The Oxford Dictionary of Islam.* New York: Oxford University Press, 2003.

———. *The Oxford History of Islam.* New York: Oxford University Press, 1999.

Fernea, Elizabeth Warnock. *In Search of Islamic Feminism: One Woman's Global Journey.* New York: Doubleday, 1998.

Fromkin, David. *A Peace to End All Peace: The Fall of the Ottoman Empire and the Creation of the Modern Middle East.* New York: Henry Holt, 1989.

Haddad, Yvonne Yazbeck. *The Muslims of America.* New York: Oxford University Press, 1991.

Hodgson, Marshall. *The Venture of Islam*. 3 vols. Chicago: University of Chicago Press, 1974.

ibn Ishaq, Musa. *The Life of Muhammad*. Translated by A. Guillaume. Karachi: Oxford University Press, 1987.

Kurzman, Charles, ed. *Liberal Islam: A Sourcebook*. New York: Oxford University Press, 1998.

Lawrence, Bruce. *Shattering the Myth: Islam beyond Violence*. Princeton, NJ: Princeton University Press, 1998.

Lewis, Bernard. *What Went Wrong?: The Clash Between Islam and Modernity in the Middle East*. New York: Oxford University Press, 2002.

Smith, Jane I. *Islam in America*. New York: Columbia University Press, 1999.

Tripp, Charles. *A History of Iraq*. Cambridge: Cambridge University Press, 2002.

Zaky, A. R. "Medieval Arab Arms." In *Islamic Arms and Armour*, edited by Robert Elgood. London: Scholar Press, 1979.

Zuhur, Sherifa. *Revealing Reveiling: Islamist Ideology in Contemporary Egypt*. Albany: SUNY Press, 1992.

INTERACTIONS

Allison, Robert J. *The Crescent Obscured: The United States and the Muslim World, 1776–1815*. New York: Oxford University Press, 1996.

Ambrose, Stephen E., and Douglas G. Brinkley. *Rise to Globalism: American Foreign Policy since 1938*. New York: Penguin, 1997.

Austin, Allan D. *African Muslims in Antebellum America: Transatlantic Stories and Spiritual Struggles*. New York: Routledge, 1997.

Bornstein, Erica. *The Spirit of Development: Protestant NGOs, Morality, and Economics in Zimbabwe*. Stanford, CA: Stanford University Press, 2005.

Bull, Narcus. "Origins." In *The Oxford Illustrated History of the Crusades*, edited by Jonathan Riley-Smith. New York: Oxford University Press, 1995.

Bulliet, Richard. *America and the Muslim World—A Series of Five E-seminars*. Columbia University Digital Knowledge Ventures, 2004. http://ci .columbia.edu.

Columbus, Christopher. *The* Libro De Las Profecias *of Christopher Columbus: An* en face *edition*. Translated by Delno West and August Kling. Gainesville: University of Florida Press, 1992.

Daniel, Norman. *Islam and the West: The Making of an Image*. Oxford: Oneworld, 1997 (1960).

Diouf, Sylviane A. *Servants of Allah: African Muslims Enslaved in the Americas*. New York: New York University Press, 1998.

Esposito, John. *The Islamic Threat: Myth or Reality?* New York: Oxford University Press, 1992.

Gomez, Michael A. *Exchanging Our Country Marks: The Transformation of African Identities in the Colonial and Antebellum South.* Chapel Hill: University of North Carolina Press, 1998.

Greene, Molly. *A Shared World: Christians and Muslims in the Early Modern Mediterranean.* Princeton, NJ: Princeton University Press, 2000.

Hahn, Peter. "National Security Concerns in U.S. Policy toward Egypt, 1945–1956." In *The Middle East and the United States: A Historical and Political Reassessment*, edited by David W. Lesch. Boulder, CO: Westview Press, 2003.

Halliday, Fred. *Islam and the Myth of Confrontation.* London: I. B. Tauris, 1995.

Housley, Norman. "The Crusading Movement: 1274–1700." In *The Oxford Illustrated History of the Crusades*, edited by Jonathan Riley-Smith. New York: Oxford University Press, 1995.

Mueller, John. *Policy and Opinion in the Gulf War.* Chicago: University of Chicago, 1994.

Nickel, Helmut. "A Crusader's Sword: Concerning the Effigy of Jean d'Alluye." *Metropolitan Museum Journal* 26 (1991).

Ninkovich, Frank. *The United States and Imperialism.* Oxford: Blackwell, 2001.

Riley-Smith, Jonathan, ed. *The Oxford Illustrated History of the Crusades.* New York: Oxford University Press, 1995.

Rubinstein, Amnon. *The Zionist Dream Revisited: From Herzl to Gush Emunim and Back.* New York: Schocken, 1984.

Seltzer, Robert M. *Jewish People, Jewish Thought: The Jewish Experience in History.* New York: Macmillan, 1980.

Siberry, Elizabeth. "Images of the Crusades in the Nineteenth and Twentieth Centuries." In *The Oxford Illustrated History of the Crusades*, edited by Jonathan Riley-Smith. New York: Oxford University Press, 1995.

Tripp, Charles. *A History of Iraq.* Cambridge: Cambridge University Press, 2002.

Watt, W. Montgomery. *The Influence of Islam on Medieval Europe.* Edinburgh: Edinburgh University Press, 1972.

MUSLIM PERCEPTIONS OF NON-MUSLIM WESTERNERS

Ahmed, Leila. *A Border Passage.* New York: Penguin, 1999.

al-Jabarti, Abd al Rahman. *Napoleon in Egypt: Al-Jabarti's Chronicle of the French Occupation, 1798.* Princeton, NJ: Markus Wiener, 1997.

bin Laden, Osama. *Messages to the World: The Statements of Osama bin Laden.* Edited by Bruce Lawrence. New York: Verso, 2005.

Hay, Stephen, ed. *Sources of Indian Tradition*. Vol. 2: *Modern India and Pakistan*, New York: Columbia University Press, 1988.

Khan, Syed Ahmad. "The Importance of Western Education." In *Sources of Indian Tradition*. Vol. 2: *Modern India and Pakistan*, edited by Stephen Hay. New York: Columbia University Press, 1988.

Rushdie, Salman. *The Satanic Verses*. New York: Viking, 1988.

NON-MUSLIM WESTERN PERCEPTIONS OF MUSLIMS

Alighieri, Dante. *The Divine Comedy*. Translated by Henry Francis Cary. New York: Thomas Y. Crowell & Company, 1897.

Belt, Don, ed. *The World of Islam*. Washington, DC: National Geographic, 2001.

Benjamin, Roger, ed. *Orientalism: Delacroix to Klee*. Sydney: Art Gallery of New South Wales, 1997.

Bourguignon, Erika. "Vienna and Memory: Anthropology and Experience." *Ethos* 24, no. 2 (June 1996).

Dowling, Ralph Edward. "Rhetorical Vision and Print Journalism: Reporting the Iran Hostage Crisis in America." PhD diss., University of Denver, 1984.

Edwards, Holly, ed. *Noble Dreams, Wicked Pleasures: Orientalism in America, 1870–1930*. Princeton, NJ: Princeton University Press, 2000.

Hourani, Albert. *Islam in European Thought*. Cambridge: Cambridge University Press, 1991.

Kahf, Mohja. *Western Representations of the Muslim Woman: From Termagant to Odalisque*. Austin: University of Texas Press, 1999.

Key, Francis Scott. "Song." In *Poems of the Late Francis Scott Key, Esq*. New York: Robert Carter & Brothers, 1857.

Lippmann, Walter. *Public Opinion*. New material ed. New Brunswick, NJ: Transaction, 1991.

Mamdani, Mahmood. *Good Muslim, Bad Muslim: America, the Cold War, and the Roots of Terror*. New York: Pantheon, 2004.

McAlister, Melani. *Epic Encounters: Culture, Media, and U.S. Interests in the Middle East, 1945–2000*. Berkeley and Los Angeles: University of California Press, 2001.

Patton, George S., Jr. "The Form and Use of the Saber." *Cavalry Journal*, March 1913.

Reeves, Minou. *Muhammad in Europe: A Thousand Years of Western Myth-Making*. New York: New York University Press, 2000.

Said, Edward. *Covering Islam*. Rev. ed. New York: Vintage, 1997.

———. *Orientalism*. New York: Vintage, 1978.

Sha'ban, Fuad. *Islam and Arabs in Early American Thought: The Roots of Orientalism in America*. Durham, NC: Acorn Press, 1991.

Shaheen, Jack G. *Guilty: Hollywood's Verdict on Arabs after 9/11.* Northampton, MA: Olive Branch Press, 2007.

———. *Reel Bad Arabs: How Hollywood Vilifies a People.* New York: Olive Branch Press, 2001.

Slade, Shelly. "The Image of the Arab in America, Analysis of a Poll on American Attitudes." *Middle East Journal* 35 (Spring 1981).

Southern, R. W. *Western Views of Islam in the Middle Ages.* Cambridge, MA: Harvard University Press, 1980 (1962).

Stockton, Ronald. "Ethnic Archetypes and the Arab Image." In *The Development of Arab-American Identity,* edited by Ernest McCarus. Ann Arbor: University of Michigan Press, 1994.

Twain, Mark. *The Innocents Abroad.* New York: Modern Library, 2003.

Van Voorst, Robert E. *Readings in Christianity.* New York: Wadsworth, 1997.

MUSLIM RESPONSES TO 9/11 AND TERRORISM

BeliefNet, ed. *From the Ashes: A Spiritual Response to the Attack on America.* Emmaus, PA: Rodale Press, 2001.

"Islamic Society of North America Denounces Terrorism in the Name of Islam," May 22, 2004, http://www.isna.net/index.php?id=35&backPID= 1&tt_news=4.

National Grassroots Campaign to Fight Terrorism, http://www.mpac.org/ ngcft/.

"Response from the Islamic Circle of North America (ICNA) to the Tragedy of September 11th," http://groups.colgate.edu/aarislam/icna.htm.

"Scholars of Islam Speak Out against Terrorism," September 17, 2001, http://groups.colgate.edu/aarislam/response.htm#Statements%20from%20L eading%20International%20Academic%20Organizations%20for%20the%20A cademic%20Study%20of%20Islam,%20Religion,%20and%20Middle%20East.

Statement by the Council on American-Islamic Relations, http://www.cair-net.org/crisiscenter/html/cair_ad.html.

POLITICAL CARTOONS

Block, Herbert. *Herblock's State of the Union.* New York: Simon & Schuster, 1972.

Damon, George H., Jr. "A Survey of Political Cartoons Dealing with the Middle East." In *Split Vision,* edited by Edmund Ghareeb. Washington, DC: American-Arab Affairs Council, 1983.

Feaver, William. Introduction to *Masters of Caricature*, edited by Ann Gould. New York: Knopf, 1981.

Fisher, Roger. *Them Damned Pictures, Exploration in American Political Cartoon Art.* North Haven, CT: Archon, 1996.

Foreign Policy Association. *A Cartoon History of United States Foreign Policy, 1776–1996.* New York: William Morrow, 1975.

Göçek, Fatma Müge, ed. *Political Cartoons in the Middle East.* Princeton, NJ: Markus Wiener, 1998.

Gould, Ann, ed. *Masters of Caricature.* New York: Knopf, 1981.

Harrison, Randall P. *The Cartoon: Communication to the Quick.* Beverly Hills, CA: SAGE, 1981.

Hess, Stephen, and Milton Kaplan. *The Ungentlemanly Art: A History of American Political Cartoons.* Rev. ed. New York: Macmillan, 1975.

Hoff, Syd. *Editorial and Political Cartooning: From Earliest Times to the Present, with over 700 Examples from the Works of the World's Greatest Cartoonists.* New York: Stravon Educational Press, 1976.

Keen, Sam. *Faces of the Enemy.* San Francisco: HarperCollins, 1986.

Kelly, Walt. "Pogo Looks at the Abominable Snowman." In *The Funnies: An American Idiom*, edited by David Manning White and Robert Abel. New York: Free Press of Glencoe, 1963.

Kemnitz, Thomas Milton. "The Cartoon as a Historical Source." *Journal of Interdisciplinary History* 4 (Summer 1973).

Mauldin, Bill. *Up Front.* New York: Henry Holt, 1945.

Michelmore, Christina. "Old Pictures in New Frames: Images of Islam and Muslims in Post World War II American Political Cartoons." *Journal of American & Comparative Cultures* 23 (Winter 2000).

Oliphant, Pat. *Oliphant!* New York: Andrews and McMeel, 1980.

———. *The Oliphant Book.* New York: Simon & Schuster, 1969.

Somers Jr., Paul P. *Editorial Cartooning and Caricature: A Reference Guide.* Westport, CT: Greenwood Press, 1998.

Walker, Rhonda. "Political Cartoons: Now You See Them!" *Canadian Business and Current Affairs* 26 (Spring 2003).

Westin, Alan F., A. Robbins, and R. Rothenberg, eds. *Getting Angry Six Times a Week: A Portfolio of Political Cartoons.* Boston: Beacon Press, 1979.

Woods, John E. "Imagining and Stereotyping Islam" In *Muslims in America: Opportunities and Challenges*, edited by Asad Husain, John E. Woods, and Javeed Akhter. Chicago: International Strategy and Policy Institute, 1996.

Index

About the Authors

Peter Gottschalk is associate professor of religion at Wesleyan University. He is author of *Beyond Hindu and Muslim* (Oxford University Press, 2000) and co-designer of "A Virtual Village" (virtualvillage.wesleyan.edu). He has lived for more than three years in India, Pakistan, and Bangladesh.

Gabriel Greenberg was born in suburban Boston, and attended college at Wesleyan University. Since graduating in 2004, he has been mainly residing in Israel, and plans to attend rabbinical school beginning in 2008.